The Fast-Food Kitchen

Sheri Torelli

HARVEST HOUSE PUBLISHERS

EUGENE, OREGON

Cover by Left Coast Design, Portland, Oregon

Cover photo © Tim Pannell/Corbis

THE FAST-FOOD KITCHEN

Copyright © 2011 by Sheri Torelli
Published by Harvest House Publishers
Eugene, Oregon 97402
www.harvesthousepublishers.com

Library of Congress Cataloging-in-Publication Data
   Torelli, Sheri, 1956-
   The fast-food kitchen / Sheri Torelli.
      p. cm.
   ISBN 978-0-7369-3039-0 (pbk.)
   1. Cookery—Planning. 2. Families—Nutrition. 3. Grocery shopping. I. Title.
   TX652.T67 2011
   641.5—dc22

2010015983

Printed in China

11 12 13 14 15 16 17 18 19 / RDS-SK / 10 9 8 7 6 5 4 3 2 1

To my husband, Tim, my cooking "guinea pig." You often tell me that a peanut butter sandwich prepared by me is better than any five-star restaurant meal. Your love and encouragement help me believe I can do anything. You have my heart! This book could never have happened without you. I love you, and I enjoy cooking for you most of all!

Acknowledgments

The many people who play a part in shaping a book enter the scene long before the manuscript is completed and the book is on the shelf. The idea for this book was born out of a desire to help busy women discover the joy that can be found in the kitchen. The original idea and title for the book came from my husband, Tim, who watched and listened as we taught seminars. Women expressed how overwhelmed they felt at mealtime because of a lack of resources, preparation, and experience. As someone who is very production-oriented, Tim knew there was a simpler, more efficient way to prepare home-cooked meals. As we began to brainstorm, talk to women in all walks of life, and ask lots of questions, *The Fast-Food Kitchen* was born. My wonderful publisher, Harvest House, believed the idea was timely, and I will be forever grateful for this wonderful opportunity.

So many others have encouraged me along this path, and I would love to let them know what their encouragement, help, and love have meant to me:

Hope Lyda, my amazing editor. She caught my vision and brought it to life. Thank you, Hope.

Shirley Almeida and Tracy Klehn—my "Paisan-Amie" girlfriends. Your love, encouragement and, most of all, your crazy fun and laughter have brightened many a day just when I needed it most.

Raquel Carlson—my close friend, and the best neighbor on earth! We tried many of the recipes in this book to determine their worthiness in terms of simple and delicious. She is a great cook for her husband, Curtis (also a great cook!), and her three sons—Andrew, Ryan, and Michael (my little loves!).

Tracey Barrett—a sweet and precious friend. She prays for me and lifts my spirits with her weekly calls of love and encouragement. I only wish we lived closer to one another!

Faithful friends of More Hours in My Day—to the women across the country who willingly and lovingly sent e-mails with their favorite recipes, you are the best! You will never know how special you are to me.

MOPS moms—your enthusiasm, your recipes, and most of all...your friendship and love!

My mom—who taught me the value of a clean kitchen and how to do it. I love you!

My nana—now in heaven, Nana was the best cook I have ever known. She could make something out of next to nothing, and she made it look so easy. She taught me that leftovers were just the beginning of a feast!

Wilma—a special treasured friend of my heart, an amazing cook, and a fabulous hostess!

Bob and Emilie Barnes—love and encouragement come so naturally for you. Your friendship means everything to me. Thank you for helping me become a maker of my home!

And saving the best for last—my children, Nicholas and Terra. You make me believe I am the best cook on earth, and I love to cook for you. Terra Bug, you will always be my favorite tea party companion! I love you both with all my heart!

❧ Contents ❧

Foreword

Emilie Barnes

I am delighted to have the opportunity to write the foreword for this book. As the founder of More Hours in My Day, I have had the privilege of meeting many women over the years who have testified how this ministry has changed their lives, but none more so than my sweet friend, Sheri Torelli. Sheri and I met in 1981 at one of my very early seminars. She was a reluctant attendee. She simply came to try to squeeze out the few extra hours in her day that she desperately needed. As a young wife and new mother, she was drowning in clutter and a disorganized home. Sheri became my "star student"! With her teachable spirit and desire to attain a level of simple organization and welcome in her home, she devoured everything I was teaching.

In the early years, Sheri edited many of our books, and as she typed our manuscripts, she was absorbing what she was reading. Many times she would try something in the book and find that it was not only very simple and easy to implement, but when it was applied, it was making a huge difference in her home and with her family. As she worked hard at becoming a maker of her home, it was not too long before others began to notice the changes.

In 1999, she began teaching seminars and traveling around Southern California and across the country, sharing what she had learned to women who were struggling as she had struggled. The principles were the same, but the stories were unique—shared from a heart that longed to see women encouraged and changed to become true makers of their own homes, whether they were stay-at-home, working out-of-home, or single women and mothers.

Today, one of the areas Sheri sees women struggling with is in the preparation of meals at home for their families. Eating out in restaurants and fast-food establishments instead of gathering around the dining room table has become commonplace, and it's almost an everyday occurrence. She recognized the need to encourage women to see the value and worth of time and energy spent in the kitchen and at the dinner table. With encouragement and help from her husband, Tim, she began formulating an idea that would provide the necessary tools and ideas to make getting back into the kitchen something to look forward to instead of dreading. And *The Fast-Food Kitchen* idea was born.

Though this book has an amazing collection of simple and delicious recipes, it is not just another cookbook. More than that, it is a book that will motivate you to personalize and utilize your kitchen, embrace methods of cooking meals that make life easier and better, and encourage your family to gather at the table more often.

Sheri shares her life-changing ideas with a realistic perspective. She fully understands the time constraints busy women and mothers face today. As you read through the pages, her ideas, recipes, tips, and stories—laced with humor and love—will encourage and delight you as you work to create a home environment that says, "Welcome home, my family. You are deeply loved!"

Emilie Barnes
Founder of More Hours in My Day and
bestselling author of more than 90 books,
including *101 Ways to Clean Out the Clutter*
and *If Teacups Could Talk*

Chapter 1

What Drives Us
to the Drive-Thru?

On this particular day, I was not thinking about how I should spend time in the kitchen or how I should change where and how my family was eating. Life was busy. My family's needs were my priority. I was juggling appointments, games, events, and regular visits to the store for everything from toilet paper to school supplies. Everything I did was in my family's best interest.

At least that's what I believed.

But on *this* day, as I was steering our car in the direction of our regular fast-food stop on the way to another activity, my daughter asked—no, *begged*—me not to have us eat out again. She just wanted a meal made and eaten at home. She was eight years old! I would like to tell you I was immediately ashamed and turned the car around to head home, but I can't, and I didn't. After all, for years I had bought into and relied upon the big lie that this lifestyle of eating out, eating on the run, and avoiding sit-down meals was the way to survive and thrive in the contemporary life. The pull of convenience and the inertia of survival mode were too much for me to halt in that one moment.

Had someone asked me why we were defaulting to drive-thru so much, I would've said that it is easier, quicker, and more economical to buy dinner than to prepare it at home. I started participating in the fast-food phenomenon. When my husband, Tim, was working as a fireman, he would be on duty for 24, 48, or sometimes 72 hours at a time. I often felt like a single mother. I had two young children, and on top of that, they were picky eaters. So I decided that it was much easier and cheaper to grab a Happy Meal (with the promise of a special toy surprise) and eat at the restaurant or in the car— no dishes and especially no whining. But it went beyond normal. Before I knew it, I was taking the kids to eat out for breakfast before school, I would grab some lunch in the drive-thru several times a week, and dinner would be fast-food most nights when Tim was on duty.

But on that day when Terra very wisely expressed her heart's simple desire, the seed for change was planted in my mind and heart. It didn't happen overnight. Old and bad habits die slowly. It was not until I acknowledged that I was wasting precious time, money, and family togetherness that changes began to occur for my family.

It took several months to incorporate manageable changes and then a couple years to perfect what I now call my *fast-food kitchen*. My energy goes toward healthier choices, faster meals (believe it or not), and investing in my family by providing a way for us to gather together now and then for meals. I thought this change would be impossible. And I thought that it was all about getting away from the fast-food establishments. But I was wrong. The small, simple steps that you and I will walk through together in this book are clearly about going *toward* a better way of living and caring for the family.

As much as I've always wanted to be a good steward of our family's resources of time, money, abilities, and provisions, I can honestly say that I've only been able to embrace this lifestyle improvement because it is so doable. There are many great reasons to start this, and many more reasons to keep doing it will emerge once you start.

To know that you can incorporate changes over time is such a relief. When I started this, nobody was timing me, scrutinizing me, or demanding that I become an apron-clad heroine. If that pressure had been there, I would've thrown up my hands in exasperation and given up. But the journey was rewarding right away, and it was a pleasure. My perspective and that of my family transformed significantly in those beginning weeks and months. That's all the motivation I needed to keep refining ways to make eating homemade meals a part of our busy lifestyle.

That's why I'm excited to share with you the tricks I have learned so that you can bypass those initial weeks when I was floundering a bit. Now you and I can walk step-by-step through these simple ideas and transform how you buy groceries, think of cooking, view mealtime, and truly support your family's best interests.

Why It's Time for the Fast-Food Kitchen

A fast-food kitchen is a homemade version of fast food in the sense that it is about efficiency, accommodating your family's needs, embracing your own preferences and style, and offering meal and snack choices for a family on the go. It won't slow you down, but it will shift how and where you spend your time and money. Instead of getting in the car yet again and driving that same stretch of road to the exit where you pull up to the window and place your order, you can walk up to your fridge, your cupboard, or your freezer and make your menu selection. You can eat at home before you go, or you can often take items with you if need be. That's flexibility at its best. And isn't that what we're craving to begin with? Isn't that probably what drove us to the drive-thru?

Make this your very own experiment and enjoy the foundation of ideas, suggestions, and proven methods that I provide. I keep the information brief and doable, and I present enough direction so you don't spend hours over the stove or with the cupboards and freezer open, scratching your head as you try to come up with something for the family to eat. It isn't like that at all. Once you have a few fast-food kitchen practices in place, you'll wonder how and why we ended up at the drive-thru window instead of our dining room window to begin with?

Along the way, you'll discover that a fast-food kitchen saves the family lots of time, energy, and money. These vital factors are no longer wasted but are considered of value… enough value to preserve and use wisely. Your time is important. Your energy is what often inspires the rest of the family. And your family's money…well, we can all relate to the need to save some dollars these days. Why should you pay for paper wrappings, disposable cups, and white bags that hold your burger for about one minute, the time it takes your ten year-old to open it and dig out the fries? When we dine out, we pay not only for food and service, but for marketing, sales, promotions, and national visibility (if you visit a fast-food chain). Those dollars would be better spent on your child's college fund, your medical bills, food to stock your shelves and freezer, and family times of pleasure (vacations, family night activities, or membership to the local pool or community center).

Who knew that small steps would lead to such a big shift toward better living? I know it now, and I can't wait for you to discover all of these things for yourself. You'll be amazed how a few decisions up front will create a domino effect of goodness. And I don't mean Domino's Pizza!

But I'm Busy…Can I Do This?

If I can do this, you can do this. And that's not just cheerleader talk. The ideas are practical and easy to implement. Once you rediscover the joys of sitting down together around the dining room table, you too will become a true believer in the fast-food kitchen. It is my hope to start a revolution of sorts—getting women excited about returning to the kitchen. As we take simple steps together, you'll be able to design a plan of action that will give you the time you desire with your family and a chance to get back into the kitchen without stress and frustration.

No matter what initially drove you to the drive-thru in the beginning, you can counter those needs and perceptions. To help you personalize your plan, I have included fast-food kitchen goals throughout the book. These will allow you to modify the steps so that they are manageable for you and your life right now. When you encounter a goal, fill in your answer(s) and then record that goal's information on the master goal page located just before the recipe section. You can refer to this master list frequently to remind you of the baby steps that lead to the freedom of a fast-food kitchen lifestyle.

With easy-to-incorporate shortcuts, I'll help you get into the kitchen and put together meals in five, ten, and 15 minutes. Using my "double-duty cooking method," you will spend no more than five or ten minutes in extra preparation time, but you'll save hours for yourself later on.

Go from Value Meals to a Valued Meal

One would think that we'd all be nutrition experts if we paid attention to the information about food, exercise, and healthy living available to us on the Internet, in the news, on TV and cable shows, and in our local gyms. But it is hard to sift through the details, and our lives are already busy enough. That's what sent some of us to the drive-thru to begin with. The fast-food kitchen is about going back to the basics of cooking and home life and personalizing those aspects of life to make life better, easier, and more fulfilling. We can approach healthy living and food in the same way.

Some family and health factors lead to extra weight, high blood pressure, diabetes, and fatigue. It isn't always because of the restaurant menu choices. But why add to these physical problems if we can ease or even reverse some of them by making changes in our homes and kitchens? You might not have an eight-year-old begging to eat at home, but you've probably heard the call to better health from all those sources I mentioned earlier. And you've probably thrown away a fast-food container thinking it should be your last bag of french fries or box with a double cheeseburger inside for a while. Most of us crave cleaner, healthier living for ourselves, and we really long for our kids to experience the same. You and I are the role models our kids have for this important, foundational factor. They will notice the choices you make, and they will eat or not eat items based on the choices you make at the store or from the menu.

I address this topic right up front because it will be good to keep in mind as you develop new methods and habits for nurturing and nourishing your family at home. This is your chance to place a high value on the meals you are preparing and you and your loved ones are eating on a regular basis.

Fast-Food Kitchen Healthy Choices

The health benefit of the fast-food kitchen is that you have control over what goes into your food, what stays out of your food, how much you make per meal, how much you serve per person, and how you and your family will go about making healthier and healthier choices as the fast-food kitchen lifestyle becomes second nature.

This isn't a diet book. You'll find casseroles and desserts listed in the fast-food kitchen recipe section. And I don't turn packaged food into a chance to make you feel guilty. I believe in convenience and finding balance. As I mentioned, the more you embrace the fast-food kitchen way of valuing food and family time, the easier it will be to choose a homemade version of a formerly packaged favorite (think macaroni and cheese) or to decide that a whole-grain bread adds more fiber for your turkey sandwich and is a better and tastier choice than the bread you used to use—the one with sugar listed as a second ingredient. It is all about awareness and the decision to care.

The choices will all be yours to make, but I guarantee you that you'll feel more in control of those choices and more prepared to make healthy changes each step of the way. Start small and with the basics. Here is a list of basics. As you read it, I know you'll nod with affirmation. They are all things we've done at one time or another or have considered doing. This is a great opportunity—the perfect opportunity—to commit to a few of these healthy changes.

1. Decide which of these are the most important for you and your family's health right now:

   - Reducing calorie intake because of weight concerns
   - Limiting sodium intake for overall health
   - Reducing sugar intake because of weight, dental health, family history of diabetes, or other reasons
   - Increasing fiber for weight loss and better digestion
   - Limiting unhealthy fats
   - Watching the amount of caffeine
   - Reducing preservatives and unnatural ingredients
   - Cutting out expensive choices like soda, sugary snacks, or too many stops at the coffee shop

2. Read labels and make healthy decisions based on the values you decided on in #1.

3. Go through your cupboards and pick and choose some packaged foods that will stay for this value shift and some that you are ready to part with.

4. Talk to your family and find out what their health goals are. See if they want to make additional modifications.

5. When you prepare a meal, make it balanced by serving grains, vegetables, and the main course, or by making the grains and vegetables as part of the entrée.

6. Watch those serving sizes. You can even buy smaller plates. When there is less space to fill, there is less desire to overdo the portions.

7. Reduce the treks to restaurants by planning ahead for the week's snack and meal needs.

8. Limit how much you are buying in the aisles of your grocery store that offer 100 percent packaged food options.

9. Consider buying local at farmers' markets so that you introduce fresh foods to your family's meal choices. They'll discover just how rich and tasty a tomato really is!

10. Make meals at home! Keep reading *The Fast-Food Kitchen* and adopt new ways of doing things so that the value of every meal becomes worthy of your family's time, health, energy, and well-being.

My Personal Fast-Food Kitchen Goal #1

During this next month, I will place value on my family's health by doing the first item on the healthy changes list. I will also choose a healthier life by doing the following four others from the list: #_____, #_____, #_____, and #_____.

Women in all walks of life—working, single, and stay-at-home—will benefit from the simple and practical solutions to the age-old question, "What's for dinner?" In the following chapters you will find motivating ideas that let you begin today! It will take some practice at first, but before long you will become efficient and master the time you spend in the kitchen.

This might be your day like my day when I heard a still, small voice redirect me back home. Actually, it was the restless, direct voice of my daughter in the backseat; but nonetheless, that was my day to begin considering how and why life needed to change. And it was the beginning of my path to the fast-food kitchen. Let this be your day and your turning point. You won't look back with an ounce of regret, only forward with a heart full of gratitude.

So pull out your apron and get ready to have some fun!

Chapter 2

There's No Place Like Home

The table was set. Everything was ready and waiting. The kitchen window was open, and a light breeze was blowing as the sun filtered through the curtains and spilled onto the dining room table. The meal was simple, a big pot of beans and homemade cornbread. I had come home from school for lunch—something I did not normally do. My entire family was there…my mom, my dad, both my sisters, and my little brother. I had no idea that my dad had been laid off from his job and that we couldn't afford to buy lunch. All I knew was that it was great to be home and together with my family around the table. We chatted, laughed, and had a great time. Before I knew it, it was time to walk back to school. I recall feeling so grounded and good for the rest of the day because of that connection with my family.

Thankfully, my dad's job status changed quickly, and back to work he went, but the recollection of those few afternoon lunches is still a sweet memory today. This pleasurable memory encouraged me as I started to create the philosophy, the plan, and the elements of what I would eventually call my fast-food kitchen.

One of the things I enjoy doing once in a while is sitting down and watching a very old show from the '50s and '60s on cable television. Life seemed so much simpler then, simply because it was. There were not as many distractions from family, faith, and traditions. And here's one thing you will notice in almost every show: Mealtimes were special. Moms took pride in their cooking abilities. Every meal was an event. People even dressed for the occasion. Dinnertime was a chance to reconnect as a family and find out what was going on in everyone's lives and what was special about their day. The dining room table was the place to be.

Mealtimes are an important part of family life. This has been true since time began. Even the Bible records many events and stories around a meal. Time around the table is important for more than just eating. Our mealtimes can become a special experience again, something to look forward to. The kitchen is the place to be. It is truly the hub of the home. There is so much more going on there than just cooking. Important teaching happens in the kitchen as well. Lessons on manners or character issues can be easily discussed while washing the dishes or measuring ingredients for a recipe or special dessert. And much can be learned from simple discussions about life while chopping vegetables or mixing pancake batter. A woman shows her love to family and friends from the kitchen. This may seem an outdated notion to you, but it is nonetheless true. The effort and heart put into a meal or a special dish speaks volumes to those who enjoy it.

I am a Southern girl. I was born in Tennessee and still have lots of family residing in Tennessee and Mississippi. When we travel back home to visit, I take a walk back in time. Many of my relatives still cook from scratch, and mealtime is truly an event. Most of my extended Southern families were farmers and ranchers. In order to run the farm efficiently, many hands were needed, and the body needed proper nourishment and energy. Hearty meals were a necessity. My great-aunts would cook and serve meals fit for a king. There would be several main dish meats, assorted vegetables and fruits, breads, cakes, and pies to delight even the pickiest tastes. Food was set out like a banquet. Breakfast was the most important meal and very hearty. It would need to sustain the men for several hours of very hard labor. Dinner (what we call lunch) was equally hearty in selection and quantity. Supper was generally made up of leftovers from both breakfast and dinner.

These women worked very long and hard preparing and serving meals to their families. They took great pride in meal preparation. It was how they showed their love and appreciation for all the hard work the men accomplished.

The Five-Aisle Dash

Now fast-forward to today. Boy, how times have changed. We are lucky to sit down to one meal a day together as a family. We eat too many meals out of a bag while driving from one activity to another. We don't even need to mention the nutritional implications of fast food and dining out as a way of life.

Because of my past delights with the tradition of nourishing, fulfilling meals, I've always been fond of the idea of being in the kitchen…wearing a cute apron as aromas fill the house with smells that would make your mouth water. The dining room table would be set with my best china, candles, and fresh flowers setting the mood. My family would be eagerly awaiting my latest epicurean delight!

Notice I mention that I was *fond* of the idea of being in the kitchen. I didn't say I was fulfilling this version of offering those in my home a meal that adds value to their day, bodies, and to the value of the family as a unit.

What happened more often than I care to remember is this scenario (maybe you've experienced it a time or two): I'm busy working on a project or shuttling a child home when I notice that it is already 5:15 in the evening. My heart races a bit. This is becoming the norm, but mealtime still fills me with slight dread. I rush to the store parking lot where I try to beat the other panicking mothers for one of the last parking spaces. I hurry in and begin my aisle roaming and rushing here and there, trying to imagine what I need and how to make the most of the last few seconds before I'm supposed to be somewhere else.

I can't remember what is already in my cupboards, so I throw in extra jars of spaghetti sauce and soup without realizing that I have duplicates of these items on my second shelf at home. After a few minutes in the store, I still only have bits and pieces of a possible meal, so I scan a couple more of the most-visited five aisles to come up with something that I could throw together in just a few minutes that will resemble a meal.

When I finally reach the cashier, I'm astounded that my few items actually turned into a cart full of stuff and a final tally that is the equivalent of a week or two's worth of groceries. An amount I'm not prepared for, so I find myself stressed as my bank card is swiped and I do the math of how little is left in our account now for other family needs.

I hurry home. I toss items into the fridge and the cupboard. I berate myself for buying the duplicate items, yet again, and then I go to work trying to present something well balanced. Or any version of a meal! I quickly settle for whatever is easiest.

Update Cooking for Your Life's Needs

This frenzied shopping and food preparation started to bother me. Even before my daughter pointed out how ridiculous our situation had become, I was longing to have a bit of that peace and comfort of my childhood days of Southern living. Learning to cook was quite natural for me. Not everybody has that background, but a lot of us know the basics, and we're not doing those either. That was my situation. Life unfolds in a way that is unique to you, and cooking and meal preferences become unique.

When I grew up, I married a wonderful Italian man who liked to eat quite differently from my family. My cooking skills were challenged the minute we said, "I do!" This new husband of mine didn't like cheese, butter, sour cream, mayonnaise, dressings, and so on. I think you get the picture. If you know anyone from the South, you realize that the first word of most recipes names is "fried"—and they're almost always served with gravy or sauce on top! So I had to learn a new way of cooking.

The repertoire of meals I was good at preparing now had to be re-created. I was used to cooking for a family of six. Now it was just him and me. As a very young wife, I really wanted to please my husband and make food he would enjoy, but I soon realized that he wouldn't eat anything I had learned how to cook. So I had to start from scratch all over again. This is where many of you find yourselves. You don't have the knowledge, the skills, the proper tools, or the time to create meals that could be featured in a Martha Stewart or Rachael Ray magazine. You have picky eaters, a schedule that would frustrate a Wall Street executive, and a budget that is already stretched to the max.

That's why the fast-food kitchen is perfect for you!

All you need is a desire to show love to your family in the kitchen. A desire that is born out of devotion to the people God has placed in your family and the difference you can make just by cooking at home. Update your view of cooking. Dust off those images that you'd like to strive for from your childhood, and get rid of those images that don't fit with your current lifestyle or your family's particular needs. Make your fast-food kitchen a place that serves you and your goals.

My "credentials" are simple. I have known what it is like to cook for two while working outside the home, I have cooked for my family as a working mom, stay-at-home mom, owner of a home-based business for many years, and as a caregiver for my father-in-law. But it was not until I became the caregiver that I realized that all my effort over the years to be an organized life and home manager were coming together in a wonderful way. It took this situation for me to realize how valuable these skills are to me and my family.

When my father-in-law, Luther, came to live with us, he was a very sick man. He was in the final stages of Alzheimer's and was a diabetic. He lived with us for two years and required constant round-the-clock care. He had to be fed, bathed, diapered, and dressed, and his meals had to be prepared in a very specific manner. As a diabetic he was unable to eat certain foods but had to have a very balanced diet. It was challenging to say the least.

I really struggled to figure out how to cook well-balanced meals for very selective eaters, save time on cooking and cleanup, and come up with new, delicious recipes that would fit into my budget. At times I was frustrated and wanted to throw in the dishtowel. My lack of training and knowledge coupled with the stresses of not enough time or money made me a cranky mom. I scoured magazines looking for new ways to make hamburger appealing to my family. Nothing I made ever came out looking like it did in the magazine.

As I faced the new challenge of caring for someone who had a strict dietary requirement, I began to see how my early teaching and training was beginning to really make a difference. I had some basics down—but I also knew I still had a lot to learn. I am still learning to this day. I was helping my father-in-law stay well nourished but along the way I was learning skills that have changed my family's relationship to food and to each other. These are the skills I've learned through trial and effort, and I can't wait to share them.

What Is in Your Memory Cupboard?

Did your family grow up using the kitchen for cooking or as a hallway to the other part of the house? Were you introduced to the delight of food and meals, or did you see it as a necessity or maybe even as a forbidden joy? Open up your food memory cupboard and consider how food was prepared, discussed, or presented in your home. That might tell you a lot about how you use it, view it, and serve it to your family.

Many women today didn't have moms who taught them the basics in the kitchen because many of these mothers were also working outside the home. It takes time and practice to become an efficient, confident cook when the example was not set for you in the earlier years. And for those of us who did see that cooking was fulfilling and worthwhile, we don't just inherit the genes. It still takes time, the effort to gain knowledge, and the proper tools. Rest assured, each necessary ingredient for the fast-food kitchen way of life can be learned in baby steps.

Let's find the time we need to order our kitchens into functioning places filled with aromas that take us back in time to memories of meals around the dining room table. There is a better way to tackle the overwhelming task of providing meals and memories for our families. We can save time and money by cooking and eating at home. We can provide well-balanced and easy-to-prepare meals, and we can save time while doing it. And every minute saved in the kitchen is time that can be spent doing things that matter, such as reconnecting with the family you love.

My Personal Fast-Food Kitchen Goal #2

I will be willing to take baby steps now and in the following weeks. My goal is to make the following three changes to the way I approach food, cooking for my family, and my kitchen:

1.

2.

3.

Keeping Special Occasions Special

It was one of those amazing Southern California summer days at the beach—a breezy afternoon—warm, but not too warm. I spent the day with my sister and a couple of friends. Tim (then my boyfriend) and I walked up and down the beach hand in hand, and we dreamed of living there someday. After a great day, we went home, and I got ready for a date later that evening. Tim picked me up around 7:00, and we drove back down to the beach to a beautiful five-star restaurant, the Reuben E. Lee, an old ship-turned-restaurant docked in the harbor in Newport Beach. I felt so grown up (we were both 19) to be having dinner with my boyfriend at such a lovely place. We were seated in the middle of the restaurant at a beautiful candlelit table, fresh flowers, white linens, crystal glasses, and fine china. We carefully ordered our dinner and thoroughly enjoyed each course. Soft music played in the background. Sometime after dinner and before dessert, my handsome, adorable boyfriend slid out of his chair and down onto one knee and asked me to be his wife. The moment was perfect. As I said yes, he slid the most beautiful ring on my finger. We kissed, and everyone in the restaurant clapped and cheered for us. We have been married nearly 34 years, and that day is as clear as if it happened yesterday. What a celebration!

I would venture to guess that you have special memories of going out to dinner as a family for a special occasion or celebration. Perhaps it was for a birthday or anniversary. It might have been the announcement of a new baby or job promotion. Maybe you celebrated the end of the school year and a good report card. Whatever the occasion, it was special.

There was a time when eating out—even lunch at McDonalds—was a special treat. The problem now is that eating out has become so commonplace that it is no longer special or a celebration. It is a bad habit—and a very costly one! Embracing the fast-food kitchen will help you put eating out at restaurants into perspective.

When dining out is preserved as a special event, it creates the opportunity to get dressed up, to create a sweet memory, to try something new, and to celebrate something special happening in your family.

My Personal Fast-Food Kitchen Goal #3

I will change the way I view eating out. I will save eating at _____ restaurant for the following upcoming occasion or celebration: _____ .

We need the fast-food kitchen today more than ever before. We move at a frenetic pace with lifestyles that are crazy busy. We need to take advantage of the many gadgets and time-savers we have in our homes and begin to make them work for us. Many women today are working out of the home and have physically fewer hours at home than their stay-at-home counterparts.

Chapter 3

What Is the Fast-Food Kitchen?

The fast-food kitchen is a well-run kitchen where planning is the key to achieving success, and efficiency is the reward. All food supplies, as well as utensils and equipment, are stored for easy accessibility. Meal planning and "double-duty cooking" (which I'll explain later), are paramount to achieving the desired outcome—preparing and serving meals in 15 minutes. When your utensils, pots, pans, and dishes are arranged to allow you to get in and move efficiently around your workspace, the goal of preparing and serving balanced meals quickly is attainable. No matter what space you have to work with, your kitchen can run like a well-oiled machine.

If you had your dream kitchen, what would it look like? I have a lovely kitchen that my husband, Tim, designed for me shortly after we moved in. I have lots of counter space, and it is organized to fit my cooking lifestyle. But if money and square footage were no object, my dream kitchen would be at least the size of two large master bedrooms. It would have a huge walk-in pantry with an additional refrigerator/freezer. There would be a kitchen island with room on all sides for at least three people to move about comfortably. The island would be equipped with a small sink and plenty of electrical outlets. My dream kitchen would have the latest and greatest appliances, and there would be space for everything to fit comfortably inside cabinets so my counters could be virtually clear.

Likely, your dream kitchen would look different from mine, and yet we would have many of the same wants and desires. We all like the idea of spacious, efficient, clutter-free areas where it doesn't take an act of Congress to retrieve what we need when we need it. But we can have efficient kitchens that work with the space we have and keep it running smoothly.

Say Goodbye to the Ineffective Kitchen

Now that we've enjoyed a good daydream about the ultimate cooking space, let's address the nightmare kitchen. Unfortunately it is the one that many of us start with before we roll up our sleeves and put in some dedicated time to organizing and transforming it into something better. These are easy to spot because they become the catch bin for everything, especially those items that don't seem to have an official "home."

Most homes have well-used entrances that lead people near or directly through the kitchen. This encourages a lazy routine for every family member to come in and dump everything on the counters and table. Things get shoved into nooks and crannies. Papers are stacked and moved all over the kitchen. Then we shuffle those piles of paper around the house, and soon they turn up back in the kitchen. Remember, the kitchen truly is the heart of the home…but sometimes it's also the heap of the home!

In order to begin utilizing our kitchen workspace in a systematic way, you will have to make some changes. The fast-food kitchen will move smoothly once we get it into shape. It won't take long if you work diligently each day, spending 15 to 30 minutes toward getting it organized and accessible. Just as clutter in other areas of our home keeps us distracted and stressed, the same is true of the kitchen. I truly believe more women would spend time in the kitchen if they could walk in and start cooking. But the thought of pouring through piles of papers or dishes with no end in sight is overwhelming. No need to be defeated before we start…so let's make sure that doesn't happen.

Creating a Fast-Food Kitchen

The first basic rule of successful organizing is that there are only so many hours in a day, and you need to maximize those hours with good time management. As I mentioned earlier, set a goal that is reasonable for you to accomplish. A goal should push you a bit, but it is really meant to work for you and not against you! Congratulate yourself for taking this on and be kind to yourself as you determine how much time you want to devote to this change each day.

My Personal Fast-Food Kitchen Goal #4

I will create an efficient, pleasant space by taking simple steps and spending _____ minutes a day for _____ weeks to shape my personalized fast-food kitchen.

Together we can explore the things to do and things not to do as you start shaping your fast-food kitchen. I'm offering suggestions based on my experience and my family's experiences and needs. You might have special circumstances or preferences. Just modify as you go. An efficient kitchen won't be of any use to you if it is set up for how someone else works!

Get the number one tool for success. The number one "tool" you need in your kitchen is a reliable digital timer. Yes, it is handy when timing the baking of a cake, but I'm suggesting it as your number one tool to keep you organized. What daily time allotment did you decide on for your recent goal? Set the timer accordingly and get to work! If you're like me, you'll be surprised when the timer goes off—you'll want to keep on working! You might modify your covenant after the first few days in case you were overly or under ambitious. But then stick to whatever you've decided.

A timer allows you to stay on task and not become distracted. I love to joke that I am a really spontaneous person, but the reality is that I am just easily distracted. If you are a mother with small children, I can assure you that you are easily distracted as well. Using a timer keeps me on task and helps me to work fast.

Just get started. Don't get overwhelmed by the big picture. Your task today isn't to accomplish that. Today, your task is simply to set your timer and take a step toward the big picture. Begin with one small area and work fast to clear out, clean, and put back what belongs in a given drawer, cabinet, or shelf. For example: Set the timer for 15 minutes and completely empty your utensil drawer. Rinse out any dividers or containers and quickly wipe dry. Wipe out the drawer with a damp cloth and then replace the utensils you use most often. You don't need 20 wooden spoons. Five or six good quality wood, bamboo, plastic, and metal spoons will serve you well.

- Keep like items stored together.
- Store lesser used items in the back of the drawer.
- Store those items you use often in the front of a drawer or cupboard.

Use this method throughout your kitchen. It may take a few weeks to completely get your kitchen in working order, but it will be well worth the time invested.

Get rid of what doesn't belong. You'll be surprised once you start looking closely at your kitchen how many items that add clutter are elements that don't even belong in a kitchen! It is eye-opening. So grab a box or reusable grocery bag and start gathering all those items that belong in other rooms of the house. Watch for papers, books, backpacks, bills, magazines, and tools that belong in the garage and not in the kitchen.

Turn to resources that will inspire your changes. Peruse your local bookstore or look online to see what books are out there that might suit your particular emphasis of change. If anything seems like a good fit, add one or two of them to your personal library. In the book I coauthored with Emilie Barnes, *More Hours in My Day*, we strive to encourage manageable change. In chapter 15, we specifically address "Total Mess to Total Rest," which provides ways to de-clutter and organize your kitchen. See which resources can help you implement the changes you're ready to make.

Call on a friend for support. Any time you are de-cluttering, it usually is a good idea to invite a friend to help you make tough decisions. And make sure you don't invite a sentimental packrat to be your support and helper. You need someone who can be reasonable but strong. They can help you talk through different possibilities and brainstorm solutions for clutter concerns or organization options. A good friend also adds laughter and cheer to the experience. What could be better?

Pass it on. As you take inventory of what you have, you will find many items in the kitchen that you no longer want or need. If they are still in good shape, don't throw them away. You can bless a young couple starting out by giving them items you are no longer using. Or donate to your church's rummage sale, the local Salvation Army, Goodwill, or some other nonprofit organization. Before I donate anything, I always check with my neighbor to see if she needs or wants any of my giveaway items. Sometimes she is able to use what I have, and sometimes she doesn't have a need for a particular item.

Same goes when you come across multiples of particular items. If you've stocked up on flower vases for the past 12 years, pick and choose your favorites and let the rest be used and enjoyed—and stored!—by someone else.

A warning: Be careful "saving" items for a garage sale. The items take up space and cause clutter in other areas. I suggest saving items for a garage sale only if you already have a date scheduled. Otherwise, just get rid of it.

You have to decide to get ruthless and let common sense prevail. If you haven't used an item in more than two years, get rid of it—give it away or throw it away. Do it quickly and don't look back. Remember Lot's wife in the Bible!

Fix it or let it go. If you have appliances or utensils that you keep moving from counter to counter or shelf to shelf because you plan to "someday" have them fixed, it is time to throw them away or donate them to an organization that allows residents, students, or employees to repair them for the experience or to earn extra cash. But don't keep them for a prolonged amount of time with the hope that "someday" you or a family member will take it in for repair. That day will never come.

Arrange and organize to suit your habits. Once you get everything you don't need out of the kitchen, find a convenient place for everything that remains. This will take some trial and error, but you'll love the first time you open a drawer and it holds only those items you use regularly.

Place your dishes, cookware, pots, and pans in such a way that you are not crossing back and forth to get what you need. Most used items need to be at eye level in your cabinets. If you use your Crock-Pot often, give it a shelf where the least amount of bending or stretching must take place to retrieve it. Don't place it in the back of a bottom cabinet. If you do that, you will be less likely to use it. Don't place it on a high shelf that requires a stool or ladder to get it.

If you have one particular counter where most of your preparation takes place, it only makes sense to keep the items you most often use close by and easy to reach.

Stock up on the basics. You will need to have your pantry (or wherever you store your food items) organized and functional. In the next chapter, I'll provide you with a sample list of basic items that need to be in your pantry. Some of the items will vary, but this will give you a starting point.

Make things easy for your future meals. Make up a basket with paper goods that you leave out on the counter. Fill it with paper plates, napkins, cups, and plastic silverware. The silverware can be stored in the cups. When you are serving a "fast-food" meal, you can set the basket on the table so that each person can reach it.

Let the fun begin. Once you get your kitchen down to the basics of just exactly what you need and will use, you will begin to get excited. Having roomy shelves and drawers to store kitchen equipment is so much easier than spaces that are overflowing and require you to move and shuffle one stack of dishes or utensils to retrieve another stack. A well-organized and efficient kitchen is a joy forever! Okay, that may be an overstatement, but you get the picture.

My Personal Fast-Food Kitchen Goal # 5

I will clear out the clutter and the unnecessary items in my kitchen, including the following:

And I will make room for a more efficient way of cooking, eating, and living.

By using common sense and taking time to think through how you like to work in your kitchen, you can arrange it so that it functions well. A well-ordered and functioning kitchen makes it a happy place to spend time and energy. Take it slow and enjoy the process.

Chapter 4

Personalize Your
Fast-Food Kitchen

Getting in and out of the kitchen quickly takes practice, the right tools, and tips for making life easier. When our mothers and grandmothers cooked, they didn't have the luxury of computers and the Internet to go look for recipes, tips, and ideas to make their time in the kitchen more efficient. Today we have a wealth of information and ideas to help us out. This chapter will be loaded with practical, helpful, and easy-to-use ideas to make quick work of kitchen time.

Clean Efficiently

1. To pick up dry spills on your kitchen counters such as sugar, crumbs, or sprinkles, simply whisk them away with a lint roller! Glide the lint roller over those pesky crumbs, and the sticky paper will pick up every last crumb.

2. To disinfect your kitchen sponges and dishcloths, simply wet them under the faucet, wring out most of the water, and place them in the microwave oven for 30 seconds to 1 minute. The microwave will kill any germs and get rid of that mildew smell. After taking them out of the microwave, rinse under water with a little soap (if desired) and wring dry.

3. Once or twice a month, put sponges in the silverware compartment in your dishwasher for a thorough cleaning.

4. When cleaning out a cabinet, pantry, or refrigerator, use "miracle minutes" and your timer to stay on task. Clean one shelf or drawer at a time. Set the timer for 15 minutes. Empty everything from that particular shelf. Quickly wipe it down. Throw away the trash, replace what belongs, and give away any items that you no longer need but could bless someone else. You may only clean one shelf a day, but by the end of the week, you will begin to see a difference.

5. Think of your refrigerator and freezer as another closet or cabinet. Store logically, keeping what you use often easily accessible. Don't forget to use

turntables on 1–2 shelves to place small jars of condiments, jams, jellies, syrup, sour cream, cottage cheese, and other items. It makes locating and retrieving such things so much easier.

6. Line your kitchen shelves with nonskid liners and a tea towel or dishcloth on top. The liner keeps the cloth in place. As a result, your refrigerator will look attractive, and it will stay much neater. The cloths on each shelf prevent spills from traveling down onto other shelves. If something spills, simply take out the cloth and replace it with a clean one.

7. To line your kitchen shelves with greater ease, place the shelf paper in the freezer for at least a half hour before you use it. The cold from the freezer keeps the shelf paper firm, and it will roll on much more smoothly. The more smoothly it rolls on, the less bubbles and bumps will form.

Get Your Pantry Organized

1. Empty your pantry one shelf at a time and throw away any items that have expired.

2. The first step in organizing your pantry is to drag a big trash can over by the pantry. You should also have a countertop cleaned off for this exercise. Simply go through your pantry and take everything out—one item at a time. Look at the dates on the items. If it has expired or remained unused for a year, throw it into the trash. If it's still good and used regularly, put it on the counter.

3. If a food donation program is close to your home, you can put "still good but never used" items into that. But unless you're going to take the items as soon as you're finished, don't do it. These items should never go back into your pantry. If you're going to procrastinate on taking the items right away, just throw them into the trash! Don't feel guilty—you will save so much money with an efficient pantry that you will be able to make a monetary donation to charity later.

4. Be sure to check the weight of your trash regularly. Don't create a trash bag that you can't lift!

5. It should take about half an hour to throw things away or put them on the counter. If it takes you longer, you either have way too much food, or you're stressing too much over the "trash or counter" decision. You have to be ruthless. If you've never used it, it's only taking up space and keeping you from having an efficient pantry. Work as quickly as you can, and when in doubt, toss it!

6. When you put things back in the pantry, arrange them logically. If you use

canned soups, vegetables, and/or fruits every single day, they should be on the easiest shelf to reach. This is usually at eye level, so you can clearly and easily read the cans.

7. All of the canned goods should remain together. The type of cans used more than the others should be the most accessible. For example, if you use canned vegetables for dinner every night, soup occasionally, and canned fruit rarely, you should have the fruit in the back, the soup in the middle, and the canned vegetables right in front.

8. Store box mixes together by category: cake mixes, pudding, stuffing, pasta, rice, cereals, and so on.

9. Small packaged mixes such as dressings, soup, and gravy packets should be stored in a clear jar or plastic organizer.

10. Label your shelves to make finding what you are looking for and replacing items when you go grocery shopping easy. Also, your husband and children can help more easily if they know where everything belongs.

Stock Your Pantry with the Basics

Every pantry needs to have certain items on hand that are basic to cooking in the kitchen. This list is not all-inclusive, but it gives you a starting place. You may need to add or delete some items, depending on what you use.

Miscellaneous

Coffee	Canned soup	Dry pasta
Tea	Chicken broth	Bisquick
Sugar/sweeteners	Beef broth	Syrup
Flour	Canned tomatoes	Jam/jellies/honey
Cooking spray	Canned tomato sauce	Peanut butter
Olive oil		Canned tuna
Vegetable oil	Canned tomato paste	Canned olives— sliced and chopped
Canned vegetables	Bread crumbs	

Basic Spices

Baking powder	Dry onions	Salt
Baking soda	Garlic powder	Pepper
Onion powder	Garlic salt	Vanilla extract
Onion salt	Seasoned salt	Cinnamon

Appliances

Microwave oven	Coffee pot	Measuring bowls
Crock-Pot	Utensils	Wooden or bamboo spoons
Toaster or toaster oven	Can opener	Spatula
FoodSaver	Hand chopper	Serving utensils
Blender	Sharp knife set	Cake/pie server
	Measuring spoons	

Pans

Large skillet with lid	Stew/soup pot	Loaf pans
Small skillet with lid	Saucepans, 2–3 different sizes	Cookie sheet
Roasting pan with lid	Cake pans	Teapot

Once again, your list will vary depending on your storage space, as well as your cooking and baking needs. This gives you the basics and a good place to start.

My Personal Fast-Food Kitchen Goal #6

I will review the pantry basics list and will create my personal version by _____ (date). And I will plan to buy a few items each _____ until my pantry is well stocked and suits the most frequent needs of my family. These are the items I know I want to get right away:

1.   4.

2.   5.

3.   6.

Store Food Simply

When storing purchased foods or leftovers, remember the key to keeping food lasting longer: Match the size of the food you are saving/storing to the size of the container. When the container or bag is too big, you'll likely need to toss the food faster. Less space means less air, and extra air causes spoilage.

Freezer

1. When purchasing meats—beef, fish, and poultry from the grocery store— repackage them into FoodSaver or airtight bags, unless you intend to use them in the next 2–3 days. The store packaging is not airtight, and the food will develop freezer burn very quickly.

2. Freeze your nuts in sealable bags or FoodSaver bags for the freshest nuts ever!

3. As space allows, store your chips and crackers in the freezer. They will stay as fresh as the day you bought them—perfectly crisp and delicious!

FoodSaver Guidelines

1. Beef, pork, chicken, and turkey can be stored in the freezer for 2–3 years. It can be stored raw or cooked.

2. Fish can be stored for 18 months.

3. Freeze deli meats in family-size portions.

4. Sliced and block cheese can be stored in FoodSaver bags. I place a piece of wax paper between slices of cheese for easier removal.

5. Bagels store beautifully and last for 18–24 months. I flash-freeze before freezing to eliminate too much compression. Slice before you freeze for quicker thawing.

6. One tip I learned is to flash-freeze items on a cutting board in the freezer for 30 minutes before placing in the plastic bags. Because the air is completely eliminated, some items can be squeezed too much and become unable to be used as intended. This includes hamburger buns, breads, cookies, and bagels.

7. You can reseal potato chip bags, grated cheese bags, cereal bags, frozen vegetables, frozen potato bags—almost any bag that is freezer safe can be resealed to keep fresher longer.

8. I purchased several square salad-sized microwave safe plates at a discount department store. I use those to make us gourmet TV dinners. I place one serving of what I prepared for dinner on the plate. I slide it into a FoodSaver bag and seal it tight. When it is time to reheat, I take it out of the freezer, cut the bag open and place it in the microwave oven for 2 minutes on defrost, then 2–3 minutes on high.

MAKE IT LAST: THE EFFICIENT WAY TO FREEZE AND REHEAT FOOD

Flash-Freeze—Flash-freezing is simply placing food items on a cutting board or cookie sheet and placing in the freezer for approximately one hour. Flash-freezing will keep certain foods from sticking together when freezing, such as hamburger patties or chicken. Other foods need to be partially frozen to keep firm enough so as not to completely collapse when placed in a FoodSaver bag. Breads (including buns, rolls, and bagels) will flatten to the point where they would not be usable. Set the timer so you don't forget you have something in the freezer.

Refresh and Reheat—Refreshing foods is simply what you must do to reheat or reuse a food product that has been stored in the refrigerator or freezer.

- *Cooked hamburgers.* If frozen, take out of the freezer. Wrap in a damp paper towel and defrost in the microwave for one minute. Turn over and repeat if still frozen. Then cook on high for one minute. It will sizzle like you just took it off the grill. Using a damp paper towel keeps the meat from drying out. You can use the same paper towel for several patties, just re-dampen when necessary.

- *Bacon.* To reheat cooked bacon, simply place in a dry paper towel and reheat for 10–15 seconds on high in the microwave. Tip: When cooking bacon for freezing, you may want to undercook it by 30 seconds if you're microwaving it, and an extra 30–45 seconds if you're frying it in a pan. I like to store cooked bacon in food-safe bowls so they hold their shape (for sandwiches or a breakfast meal).

- *Pasta.* To refresh cooked pasta, simply place it in a strainer and pour boiling water through it. It will taste like you just cooked it! This is a trick restaurants use. You cannot freeze cooked pasta, but you can refrigerate it for 2–3 days in a regular storage bag or bowl or up to two weeks in a FoodSaver bag. Remember, cooking the pasta for recipes is the part that generally takes the most time.

- *Tortillas.* I buy handmade tortillas from Trader Joe's and their shelf life is very limited in the refrigerator. So I like to freeze them. To refresh and heat tortillas in the microwave, simply dampen paper towels (you will dampen several depending on how many you are heating up at one time) and layer the tortillas inside the paper towels, one per sheet. Heat on high for 30 seconds per tortilla (microwave heating varies, so you will have to experiment). They come out perfectly steamed. Place them in a tortilla warmer. Steaming versus frying saves time and lots of calories.

- *Pancakes.* I always cook three or four extra pancakes for a quick breakfast meal when I am in a hurry. To refresh and heat in the microwave, dampen paper towels and layer the pancakes inside, one per paper towel. If frozen, defrost for one minute and heat on high for 30 seconds. If thawed, it takes approximately 30 seconds per pancake. The damp paper towels keep the pancakes from becoming hard disks. They are moist and delicious, just as if they were fresh off the griddle.

- *Waffles.* Make three or four extra waffles and store in the freezer. To reheat, simply place in the toaster oven (or toaster) and toast. They will crisp up and taste as though they were just made.

Refrigerator

1. With the FoodSaver, you can store bagels in the refrigerator for up to four months.

2. When saved in the FoodSaver bags, deli meats and cheese last several days longer than store packaging.

3. Cooked pasta can be sealed in a FoodSaver bag for up to 14 days.

4. Seal tortillas in the FoodSaver bags to stay fresh longer.

5. Fresh, washed, and dried vegetables can be stored for a week or two.

The Three Great Appliances

I believe that these three appliances are necessities: the Crock-Pot, the microwave oven, and the FoodSaver. I could not live as efficiently as I do without any one of these amazing modern-day tools. I have two Crock-Pots that are different sizes, two microwave ovens, and my FoodSaver. I couldn't live without any of them. I use them often. Here are some quick tips to use these appliances to their fullest potential and to serve your fast-food kitchen.

1. Keep them easily accessible. This is number one! If you can grab them quickly and easily, you will be more likely to use them. Don't put them too high, too low, or behind pots and pans.

2. Check with friends for Crock-Pot recipes that their family enjoys. The Crock-Pot is a must for today's busy women. Many recipes for the oven

can be easily adapted for the Crock-Pot. We've included a number of tried-and-true Crock-Pot recipes in this book.

3. Purchase a "lamp timer" at your local hardware store to schedule exactly when you want your Crock-Pot to turn on. Some recipes call for fewer hours to cook. So while you are at work or running errands, your Crock-Pot will turn on automatically and have dinner ready when you get home.

4. Purchase some microwave-safe dishes, bowls, and pans to use in the microwave.

5. Practice cooking recipes in the microwave. It's not just for reheating. The microwave saves incredible amounts of time and energy.

6. Teach your children to use the microwave safely. It is a safe alternative to using the stove or oven, however, they need to learn the rules of the microwave: What can and cannot be cooked or reheated? Which dishes can be used for specific cooking times?

7. The FoodSaver is my favorite appliance in my kitchen. If you have one, you know exactly what I mean. The unit vacuum-seals the bag, completely keeping any air from touching your foods. Air is the enemy to foods both in the refrigerator and the freezer. The FoodSaver can be purchased at Costco, Target, Walmart, and many other stores.

Having an efficient kitchen takes planning, but once you have an organized and stocked kitchen with just what you need on hand, preparing wholesome and delicious meals will become second nature.

Chapter 5

Double-Duty Cooking
Is Twice As Good

A key component of the fast-food kitchen is to make the most out of the moments you are cooking. You might discover that you love cooking and creating new and improved meals for your family. But the initial goal is to have flexibility and freedom to not be there too long. Being efficient saves you time, money, and actual food resources. That's why double-duty cooking will greatly enhance your life.

Double-duty cooking is not a new thing. It is easy to begin, and once you practice this time-saving method, you will be amazed at what you can accomplish in five or ten minutes. Start simple and build from there. Any new task you learn must be undertaken in small, easy steps. Women who spend time in the kitchen probably already use this method, even if they call it something else. You might already be using some form of double-duty cooking in your kitchen. Simply stated, this is my definition of double-duty cooking: "Cooking an extra portion or two of what you are already cooking." When you are grocery shopping, include extras for double-duty cooking.

Anytime you can double or triple a recipe, you will save time later on. You already have the ingredients and utensils out, so why not use the time in the most productive way? The time saved will allow you to put great meals on the table in record time. When you learn to utilize "miracle minutes" in the kitchen and cook 2–3 extras of whatever you are already preparing, it sets the stage for true efficiency in the kitchen. Saving time will create pockets of possibility for fun, relationships that matter, and a very happy mom!

FAST-FOOD KITCHEN TIPS

- *Mark storage bowls.* Purchase dry-erase markers for use on plastic storage containers, food-safe bowls, or stoneware bowls. They write on the surface easily and are just as easily removed when washed.

- *Mark freezer storage bags.* Purchase permanent markers to clearly date and identify contents of your freezer bags. Most foods take on a different look once completely frozen.

- *Get the most out of chicken breasts.* Cook chicken breasts in olive oil, cool, and store 1–2 individually in FoodSaver bags; cube chicken breasts, one at a time, into bags for different meals, such as chicken salad, chicken pesto pasta, casseroles, tacos, etc.

- *Preserve your fruit.* Cut up fresh fruit and add one can of pineapple chunks or mandarin oranges (or both) with the juice to the fresh fruit. The acid in the canned fruit juice will keep the fruit fresh for several days.

- *Freeze chips, crackers, and cookies.* They will stay as fresh as the day you bought them. They do *not* get soggy. You can freeze and refreeze. Seal tight and get out as much air as possible from the bag before clipping and storing.

- *Color-code items.* Put a colored adhesive dot (available at any office supply/stationery store) on items you will need for a meal so the family will know not to use them.

- *Double up when shopping.* When you buy staple items for the pantry, such as sugar, flour, cream of chicken soup, tomato sauce, and so on, buy two the first time you shop so you will always have extra on hand. A staple item can be defined as any food product you use on a very regular basis.

Double-Duty Cooking Tips

Once you have the ingredients and cooking utensils out, it just makes sense to utilize your time well so that you get more accomplished quickly.

Package extra sets of ingredients. When measuring dry ingredients for any recipe—especially one you use often—make an extra set of dry ingredients and store them in an airtight bowl in the refrigerator until you make the recipe again. Mark the front of the bowl with a dry-erase marker to let you know what recipe the ingredients are for. I use this method for my meat loaf, pancakes, and scratch chocolate cake recipes. I generally measure out 2–3 extra sets of dry ingredients at a time. I store them in sealable bowls and keep them in the pantry or refrigerator. I can put my scratch chocolate cake in the oven in 7 minutes. I also measure extra dry ingredients for the frosting and keep those on hand. All I have to do is add eggs, milk, or oil, and I'm ready to go.

Make the most of every minute with simple tasks. When you are working on dinner and have some down time while waiting for water to boil, an oven to preheat, or something that needs watching while cooking on the stove, take those precious five or ten minutes to work on gathering or preparing ingredients for a recipe or meal later in the week.

- Chop an onion, celery, carrots, or grate cheese and store in sealed bags or bowls for a recipe later in the week.

- Prepare pasta for spaghetti and refrigerate it for later in the week. It will keep in the refrigerator for up to two weeks if stored in a FoodSaver bag or 2–3 days in an airtight bowl. To refresh cold, cooked pasta, simply pour boiling water over and through it in a strainer. Just add your sauce, and you are ready to go.

- Hard boil eggs for lunches or snacks.

- Make up tuna salad for sandwiches.

- Cook bacon and freeze for breakfast or sandwiches.

- Cut up fresh fruit for breakfast the next morning. Stir in a little lemon juice to keep fruit fresh.

TOP TEN RECIPES THAT DOUBLE OR TRIPLE EASILY

1. Chicken Enchilada Casserole
2. 1-2-3 Meat Loaf
3. Baked Chicken Strips (great for kids' lunches)
4. Chicken Pesto Pasta
5. Chicken Tenders with Trader Joe's Double Roasted Salsa
6. Crock-Pot Asian Chicken
7. Crock-Pot Chili
8. Easy Beef Stroganoff (Mock)
9. Easy Orange Chicken Fling
10. Tortilla, Meat, and Rice Pie

Each of these recipes can be frozen for a quick ready-to-heat dinner meal.

Use double-duty methods when you cook meat. Buy in bulk and separate into smaller packages—chicken, ground beef, turkey, and so on. You will save money by buying in bulk and repackaging.

- Store raw ground beef or turkey in 1-lb. packages; most recipes call for 1 lb. of meat.

- Buy bulk chicken and store the number of pieces and cuts for a family meal. Example: Two breasts, two drumsticks, and one thigh.

- Buy roasts twice the size you need for a recipe and cook the whole roast in the Crock-Pot. When it is finished, cut it in half. Serve one portion for dinner and set the other half aside in a bowl to cool. Use the second half for barbecue beef sandwiches. After the roast cools, shred it and add your favorite barbecue sauce. Store it in the refrigerator or freezer for use later in the month.

- Cook meats ahead of time and freeze whenever possible. I use this idea for hamburgers, ground beef, turkey, chicken breasts, and roasts.

- When cooking ground beef, cook 5–10 lbs. at one time and store cooked meat in 1-lb. packages. Remember that 1 lb. of ground beef equals 2 cups of cooked hamburger. Perfect for sloppy joes, tacos, and casseroles. Remember, cooking the meat is what takes the most time for many recipes.

- If making homemade meatballs for a recipe, make a double or triple batch and freeze the extras. They are so great in soups, sandwiches, and casserole dishes, and they are easy to work with.

- Purchase chicken breasts in bulk. Warehouse stores carry frozen breasts individually wrapped. These work well for Crock-Pot recipes. Cook several breasts in olive oil and freeze individually to be used for meals and recipes. Cut cooked chicken breasts into chunks and freeze 1-cup individual packages for use later in salads, soups, or casseroles.

Double your soup or chili recipe. After serving for a meal, fill 2-cup-sized resealable bowls, cool to room temperature, and then freeze. Don't fill all the way to the top. That way, you will allow for expansion (about ½ inch). It is the perfect single serving size.

Think "fast" for breakfast. When cooking pancakes, waffles, or French toast, cook 3–4 extra. It will only take 3–4 extra minutes, and you will have a breakfast meal prepared for a busy morning. Do the same with waffles or French toast. They can be reheated in the microwave or in the toaster oven.

- Extra pancakes, waffles, or French toast can become dinner for your children on a date night for you and your husband or on a night out with the girls.

- To reheat cooked pancakes, place them between a damp paper towel and put them in the microwave. Turn it on defrost for 1 minute, then 30–45 seconds on high. If frozen, double the defrost time and turn over in the middle of the defrosting time. Then microwave on high for 30–45 seconds. Microwaves will vary, so you might have to experiment a couple of times to get the time right. It will come out as though you just took it off the griddle.

- When cooking bacon, cook 4–5 extra strips. Freeze in a sealable bowl for use on a sandwich or for breakfast on another day.

- Bacon can be cooked in the microwave easily, and it tastes as good as it does when fried in a pan. Approximate cooking time is 1 minute per slice. Since microwaves vary, start out slow, and add minutes to the cooking time. Use a pan made especially for bacon cooked in the microwave. Pampered Chef has a large stone bar pan that works great for cooking bacon in the microwave.

- To defrost frozen, cooked bacon, place on a paper towel and cover with another paper towel. Cook on high for 10–15 seconds. It will sizzle and taste as if you had just taken it out of the pan.

Be your own best helper. When cooking extra portions, begin to feed your freezer with homemade "TV dinners." These are great to have on hand for busy days, an unforeseen and unexpected mini-crisis, or for evenings out.

One great example of this is my Chicken Enchilada Casserole, which you'll find in the recipe section and in my sample menu portion in the next chapter. I double the recipe and save half for another meal later in the week or month. Because I use canned chicken, the preparation is very quick and easy. But the real time-saver comes when I am able to get at least one more meal out of one recipe. This is double-duty cooking at its best. You can also make individual TV dinners instead of freezing half of the casserole. I purchased several square salad plates at Marshall's, and they are the perfect size for a TV dinner. I cut a square of casserole and put it on the plate. Then I add a scoop of Spanish rice. I slip the plate into a FoodSaver bag, seal it up, and place it in the freezer. On a night when I have to be out of the house for an activity or meeting, I simply take out one of the dinners and let it thaw on the counter. When I am ready to reheat, I cut the top of the FoodSaver bag off and place it in the microwave oven for 2 minutes. I give it a quarter turn, and I turn the microwave back on for 2–3 minutes or until completely warm through. A quick, delicious fast-food meal in under 10 minutes.

You will be grateful again and again for thinking ahead or stocking up for potential situations where you have limited time and can't cook. Think how often that happens during the week. Be your best double-duty helper, and in addition to time, you'll save your sanity too!

Build double-duty cooking into your lifestyle. Keep your meal planner handy so that as you add extra meals to your freezer, you can add them to the schedule for a meal later in the month (or next month). Once you start this practice, you'll become even more inspired to apply double-duty cooking to your rounds in the kitchen. As you see possible meal options being added to the list, you will realize that what would've been a fast-food run in the past can now be resolved by walking to your freezer. You now have simple solutions to that Wednesday night between school and church choir practice or that tricky overbooked Saturday when your family members will all be eating dinner.

My Personal Fast-Food Kitchen Goal #7

I will start practicing double-duty cooking _____ times a week for this first month. I will keep it simple so that it is not stressful, and I will strive to make it a new way of viewing and using time in the kitchen.

When you work efficiently in the kitchen and begin to master the art of double-duty cooking, you will be able to get meals to the table in as little as 5, 10, and 15 minutes—a true fast-food kitchen. The time you save adds up quickly and allows you to be in and out of the kitchen in minutes. This frees up time to spend with family and friends—those relationships and endeavors that really matter.

Chapter 6

Menus by Design

Women have been planning their meals ever since people started eating! Historically, planning meals likely grew out of necessity because ingredient options depended upon crop seasons or actual access to food sources. It wasn't a matter of perusing a grocery store aisle and retrieving items from shelves, produce bins, or even our local farmers' market. But that skill for putting together a balanced meal with what food options are at hand is still the basis of how we plan menus for our families.

Most of us who think of "menus" only as well-lit boards above the speaker on the way to the drive-thru window haven't fully tapped into the skill of meal planning. And many women today who actually cook more than they go out are still winging it because they don't take (or have) the time to plan. By not using a menu-planning system of any kind, they are building stress in their lives when they could be serving themselves and their families more effectively. Whichever camp you fall into, your life is going to get much easier as you embrace the fast-food kitchen and start making healthy, convenient, and simple choices about what to cook for your family.

If you're hesitant to add this discipline to the way you do things, I encourage you to keep reading this chapter before you make up your mind about this practice. I think the main reason most people don't plan their menus is because we tend to overcomplicate it. The main component to effective meal planning is to keep it simple! Keep in mind the following benefits of planning your meals.

If you make a meal plan and a shopping list from that plan, you will save $25–$35 a week without ever clipping a coupon or buying anything on sale. The reason is simple— when you don't have a written plan, you tend to buy food items that you will not be using in the week or two ahead. So you are overspending. It doesn't matter if you shop one week at a time or one month at a time. The same principle applies.

With a meal plan, you will shop less often—no extra trips to the grocery store. You will save time, gas, and money. I don't know about you, but I have never been good at going into the store for just one item and coming out of the store with just one item.

Your stress level decreases because you are not trying to figure out what to cook for dinner at the last minute. No grouchy mom! You can even delegate some of the responsibilities for dinner ahead of time to your older children or your husband.

It really is easy to make up menus and shopping lists, but it does take some practice to perfect it. There are as many ways to plan family meals as there are families. If we were to compare how women plan their meals, we would discover there is no magical way to do it. The intent of this chapter is to give you *my* simple version of how to plan your meals. You can adapt this idea and make it your own. And if you already have a method you are comfortable with, don't change it. Remember, "If it ain't broke, don't fix it!"

Start with Family Favorites

One of the main reasons I believe we don't make a menu is because we can't think of what to make. We make the same things over and over, but if asked what we cook, we can't come up with much. Having all your favorite meals ready to choose from will make menu planning easy.

All family members have their favorite family meals—personal comfort foods. My kids have several favorites that "only Mom can make!" When they come home for a visit, there are a couple of different dinners I will fix automatically, just because I know they love it. Most families seem to prepare the same few favorites over and over. I believe each family should have five or six "family favorites" that are easy to prepare. Try to have the ingredients on hand so at a moment's notice, you can pull something together quickly. But beyond the favorites, it's nice to have ideas for meals that are easy to prepare, include a few simple ingredients, and take just a few short minutes to fix.

Take index cards and write five simple meals your whole family enjoys. Make sure you have the ingredients on hand at all times so when you've worked late or you have to dash out the door, you can quickly pull it together and get it on the table. Here are some tips to make planning a family menu easy.

Use tools to make it simple. Create a menu planning sheet or download one from a favorite Internet site. You can also use the "Weekly Menu Planner" at the end of the recipe section on page 211.

Start with just the dinner meals. Most of us eat simply for breakfast, rotating the same 2–3 meals over and over. Lunch is usually leftovers or a quick sandwich, salad, fruit, and cheese. If you stay at home during the day, you can plan simple breakfast and lunch menus just to make sure you have ingredients on hand.

Gather recipes in one place. Get a stack of three-by-five cards, sit down after dinner one evening, and brainstorm all the meals your family enjoys—breakfast, lunch, and dinner. Fill out one three-by-five for each dish. Don't forget to include side dishes, snacks, and desserts. Below is an example of how the card could look:

FRONT OF CARD

Breakfast   ★ ★ ★ ★ ★

Lunch   Family Favorite Rating

Dinner

Dessert

Side Dish

Snack

NAME OF RECIPE/MEAL

Side Dishes

1.

2.

3.

BACK OF CARD

Ingredients:

This list is to be transferred to your regular weekly or monthly shopping list.

As your family members choose their favorites, add three-by-five cards like the example. Over the next few weeks, you will find yourself adding new cards as you remember dishes your family likes.

My Personal Fast-Food Kitchen Goal #8

This week I will select _____ favorite recipes and write them out on three-by-five cards, or I will use another system that works best with my resources and preferences. These are the three that come to my mind right away:

1.

2.

3.

Have your family rate the recipes. Don't forget to track how you rate the meal that you list on a card—1 star is okay, and 5 stars is a real family favorite. The rating system might help you to determine how often you serve that particular meal. Make this a family activity each week by reviewing the meals you've tried and having each family member serve as a meal judge, offering their input and rating for the week's servings. This can be a lot of fun, and you'll discover which meals you'll want to store up for frequent dining pleasure.

Having a chance for kids to express their views about the meals also gives you a chance to find foods that the pickiest eater will love. You might be surprised that your broccoli hater is a green bean fanatic. Healthy choices for meals can be shaped as you get a sense of your family members' taste preferences.

Start a file box or recipe management system. Once you have the cards completed, add them to your three-by-five card file box. This is a great job to delegate to a teenager who likes to help in the kitchen. You can add divider tabs with main headings for easy retrieval. The tabs might be labeled as follows:

Breakfast

Lunch

Dinner

Family Favorites

Snacks

Desserts

Side Dishes

Use technology to make it easy for yourself. If you are computer savvy, you can use technology to make your meal planner. There are so many different ways to use the computer—you will have to decide what works best for you. I like handwritten or typed cards because they are handy—no booting up the computer to take a look at a recipe. If you don't use a meal plan, you can still use the card idea. When you make a trip to the market, just grab the cards for the meals you are making to make sure you don't forget any ingredients.

Don't forget variety. Try to have a variety of meals for the month. By planning ahead one week or month, you will avoid repeating the same meals over and over. When choosing your meals, remember to have as many different colors as possible. Colorful foods are more appealing.

Make healthy food a priority. Managing portion sizes is very important for caloric and nutrient control. A fast-food kitchen is a healthy one because you have the ultimate control of the portion size from the beginning. You are in charge of the planning and cooking of the meal, as well as when you either serve or store it. Less food is wasted because you are buying only what you need. Also, everyone in the house is experiencing less waist size increases because you and your family are only eating what you need.

Explore ideas that suit your style. Research online to discover recipe websites, helpful hints, and ways to navigate quickly and efficiently around the kitchen.

Keep building your recipe selection. Try to add a new recipe at least once a month. It won't take long before you will have quite a supply of meal ideas. Ask friends who have lives similar to your own which three meals or recipes they use the most. It's great to exchange this kind of information. One simple, new meal idea or method can radically improve your fast-food kitchen selection or system.

My Personal Fast-Food Kitchen Goal #9

I will try to add _____ recipes a month to my favorites file.

Below I have provided you with one week's meal plan, the shopping list, and a couple recipes listed in the meal plan. This will show you how easy it is to create your own meal plan. Within this week's plan, I will point out which recipes are great for the double-duty cooking method (DD). Then I will describe which meals can take advantage of the stored, cooked food as fast-food meals (FF).

SAMPLE MENU
Week of: March 10

Day of Week	BREAKFAST	LUNCH	DINNER
MONDAY	Oatmeal Fruit Milk and Coffee DD ☐ FF ☐ PG ☐	K—Sandwich, Chips, Fruit Drink, Cookie (Sack Lunch) A—Soup and Roll DD ☐ FF ☐ PG ☐	Crock-Pot Roast (Beef or Pork) Veggies Bag and Rice Bag Ice Cream with Cookie DD ☑ FF ☐ PG ☐
TUESDAY	Cold Cereal Toast Milk and Coffee DD ☐ FF ☐ PG ☐	K—Sandwich, Pretzels, Fruit Cup, Cookie A—Yogurt/ Cottage Cheese and Crackers DD ☐ FF ☐ PG ☐	Salad with Dino Bites Canned Fruit String Cheese DD ☐ FF ☐ PG ☐
WEDNESDAY	Pancakes (make 4 extra) Bacon (make 4 extra) Bananas DD ☑ FF ☐ PG ☐	K—Sack lunch A—Turkey Sandwich with Lettuce and Cheese, Fruit DD ☐ FF ☐ PG ☐	BBQ Beef Sandwiches Chips Fruit DD ☐ FF ☑ PG ☐

DD = Double-Duty Cooking   FF = Fast-Food Meal   PG = Use paper goods   K= Kids   A= Adults

THURSDAY	Yogurt Toast Fruit DD ☐ FF ☐ PG ☐	K—Lunchables or Cafeteria A—Lunch Out DD ☐ FF ☐ PG ☐	Chicken Enchilada Casserole Bagged Salad Root Beer Floats DD ☑ FF ☐ PG ☐
FRIDAY	Waffles/Syrup Sliced Peaches DD ☐ FF ☑ PG ☐	K—Sack Lunch A—Leftover Chicken Enchilada Casserole DD ☐ FF ☑ PG ☐	Dinner Out for Dad and Mom K-Pancakes/Bacon DD ☐ FF ☑ PG ☐
SATURDAY	Crock-Pot Egg Casserole Canned Biscuits Fruit DD ☑ FF ☐ PG ☐	K and A—Sack Lunches or Fast- Food Restaurant DD ☐ FF ☐ PG ☐	BBQ Hamburgers Baked Beans Chips DD ☐ FF ☐ PG ☐
SUNDAY	Family Favorite Breakfast Ham and Eggs Hash Browns and Biscuits DD ☐ FF ☑ PG ☐	Gourmet Turkey Sandwiches with Cheese, Lettuce, and Avocado Pasta Salad DD ☐ FF ☐ PG ☐	Meat Loaf Mashed Potatoes Baby Carrots and Rolls Make Your Own Sundae DD ☐ FF ☑ PG ☐

Shopping List

Breads/Cereals:

Oatmeal

Cereal (2 boxes)

Bread (3 loaves)

Sandwich rolls (4)

Hamburger buns

Canned biscuits

Meats:

Bacon

Ham steak

Ground beef (5 lbs.)

Chuck roast or 7-bone roast (4 lbs.)

Frozen:

Hashbrowns

Chicken nuggets (Dino Bites)

Vegetables

Dairy:

Milk

Yogurt

Eggs (2 dozen)

Cottage cheese

Feta cheese

Produce:

Avocado

Lettuce/Bagged lettuce

Onions

Carrots

Canned Goods:

Canned fruit (3 cans)

Tuna

Enchilada sauce (2 medium cans)

Chicken

Baked beans

Chopped olives

Diced green chiles

Vegetables

BBQ sauce

Deli:

Turkey

Ham

Cheese

Lunchables (2)

Snacks:

Cookies

Chips

Pretzels

Crackers

Tortillas

Croutons

Salad dressing

Pasta salad

Ice cream

Pantry Staples

Coffee

Tea

Sugar/sweeteners

Flour

Cooking spray

Olive oil

Vegetable oil

Canned vegetables

Canned soup

Chicken broth

Beef broth

Canned tomatoes

Canned tomato sauce

Canned tomato paste

Bread crumbs

Dry pasta

Bisquick

Syrup

Jam/jellies/honey

Peanut butter

Canned tuna

Canned olives—sliced and chopped

Spices:

Baking powder

Baking soda

Onion powder

Onion salt

Dry onions

Garlic powder

Garlic salt

Seasoned salt

Salt

Pepper

Vanilla extract

Cinnamon

Tools/Utensils

Appliances:

Microwave oven

Crock-Pot

Toaster or toaster oven

FoodSaver

Blender

Coffee pot

Utensils:

Can opener

Hand chopper

Sharp knife set

Measuring spoons

Measuring bowls

Wooden spoons

Spatula

Serving utensils

Cake/pie server

Pans:

Large skillet w/lid

Small skillet w/lid

Roasting pan w/lid

Saucepans, different sizes

Cake pans

Loaf pans

Cookie sheet

Teapot

⚶ Chicken Enchilada Casserole ⚶

Prep Time: 15 minutes

Total Cooking Time: 40 minutes (oven)
or 2–3 hours (Crock-Pot)

Ingredients

3 chicken breasts, cubed, or 3 large cans
    chicken breast meat, or rotisserie chicken
2 cans (15 oz. each) enchilada sauce
12–15 corn tortillas
3 cups shredded cheese
Chopped onions (optional)
Chopped or sliced olives (optional)

Method

Preheat oven to 350°. Grease bottom of
9x13-inch casserole dish. Pour enchilada
sauce to cover bottom. Layer with tortillas,
then add chicken, more sauce, cheese, olives,
and onion (if desired). Continue with 2–3
more layers. Top off with extra cheese. Bake
casserole for approximately 30–40 minutes
or until hot completely through. Garnish
with sour cream and/or avocado slices.

May be heated in the microwave if prepared
in a glass casserole or microwave-safe dish.
Freezes well.

Can be layered in a Crock-Pot and cooked
on low for 2–3 hours (if using previously
cooked chicken). Garnish with extra cheese
before serving. Serves 8.

❧ Crock-Pot Egg Breakfast Casserole ❧

Prep time: 15 minutes

Total Cooking Time: 8 to 9 hours
in Crock-Pot

Ingredients

1-lb. bag frozen hash browns, partially
   thawed (shredded works best)
3 cups shredded cheddar or provolone cheese
   (or mixture of both)
12 large eggs
1 cup water or milk
2 tsp. salt
¼ tsp. freshly ground black pepper

Method

Generously spray the inside of the slow
cooker with cooking spray. Put half of the
hash browns in the slow cooker and spread
them out evenly. Top the hash browns with
half of the cheese. Repeat with the remaining
hash browns and cheese. In a large bowl, beat
the eggs with a whisk, then mix in the water
(or milk), salt, and pepper. Pour the egg
mixture into the slow cooker over the hash
browns and cheese. Cover and cook on low
for 8 to 9 hours. Serves 8.

Chapter 7

Creating Little Helpers

When our daughter, Terra, was just a toddler, she had a special place in my kitchen. At the end of the counter was a chair that she would stand on while watching me cook. As I prepared the family meal, she would offer encouragement and help, and she would ask lots of questions. Right above where she stood was a hanging wooden kitchen tool set. It had been a wedding gift and was used for looks more than anything else. One of the tools was a solid wooden rolling pin. It was her very favorite. She would take it off the rack and pretend she was helping me cook. When she got bored, the rolling pin became her "telephone" as she would call and talk to her aunt, her cousins, and even her grandfather who lived far away. She would share what I was doing and what a big helper she was. It is such a sweet memory for me, and it's something she barely remembers. But I believe it was the start of her quest to becoming a good cook and a person who is comfortable in the kitchen.

It is important and pleasurable to get our children introduced to the kitchen as early as possible. I know that when they are little, it can seem like so much extra work to include them, especially when you're in a hurry. But, later, when you could use a helping hand, you'll be so glad that you welcomed them into the kitchen and the process of preparing a meal.

Delegating simple kitchen jobs to a child as young as two helps to teach and train, and it starts them on a good path toward interest in cooking. And don't forget your boys. Young men and women all need cooking skills for their single years, and they could use what they learn from you so that they can do their share when they get married.

Welcoming Kids of All Ages to the Kitchen

Developing little helpers takes a lot of patience and work. It takes time to explain what you are doing, but the time invested will reap huge rewards. When children are young, they want to mimic everything they observe Mom and Dad doing. Because of this, the kitchen becomes a natural teaching zone. Repetition and consistency are key in helping your children learn kitchen skills. Let them ask lots of questions. Curiosity is a great teaching tool. By teaching and training them at an early age, you are creating little helpers that will become great resources to you in the kitchen as they grow older.

Some moms might wonder why they should delegate. Explaining how to do something does take a bit longer than doing it oneself—okay, sometimes a *lot* longer. But a fast-food kitchen is an efficient one, and one of the most effective ways to be efficient is to delegate. Little helpers become great time-savers when we give them the necessary tools and skills to assist us in a way that gets us in and out of the kitchen quickly.

Each child's ability and skill development differs, but the jobs below will give you an idea of what you can begin teaching your children at different ages. Start slowly and work on something until they have it mastered. Then move on to something new. It won't be long before your little helpers are an important part of your fast-food kitchen.

And moms, just because we are talking about the kitchen, don't think only about your daughters. Kids today are out on their own longer before settling down. And boys need to learn their way around the kitchen too. My son, Nick, moved out of our home when he was just 18 years old. After one of his early visits to the grocery store and the sticker shock that followed, he learned how to watch for bargains and to comparison shop. Out of necessity, he learned his way around the kitchen quickly.

Growing up, his role in the kitchen was more casual observer than participant; however, he was watching and learning. He now lives in New York and has become quite a good cook. He isn't afraid to experiment and has even taught me a thing or two!

2- to 4-Year-Old Little Helpers—Jobs They Can Do

A simple and incredibly handy trick to ease the little ones into the kitchen routine is to set aside a low drawer or bottom shelf somewhere in the kitchen where you can store a few plastic bowls, measuring cups, wooden spoons, and other cooking tools. Keep it near where you will be working, but not underfoot. When you are cleaning and cooking in the kitchen, your toddler can be nearby "cooking and cleaning" with you. As they observe what you are doing, they will try to mimic you. Encourage them with praise and don't forget to ask questions and give instructions as they are working. Child's play is actually teaching and training skills, even at this very young age. Here are some more jobs for this age group.

- Watch what you are doing while standing or sitting on a chair nearby.
- Put items in the trash can.
- Help you carry the trash to the outside trash can.
- Help you pour ingredients into a bowl or pan and then help to stir.
- Watch you load or unload the dishwasher as you explain what you're doing.
- Bring their dishes from the table to the kitchen.

4- to 8-Year-Old Little Helpers—Jobs They Can Do

- Retrieve measuring cups, mixing bowls, and kitchen tools.

- Gather items from refrigerator and pantry as directed.
- Help measure and pour ingredients into mixing bowls and pans with supervision.
- Mix the ingredients with your help.
- Grease and flour pans for baking.
- Help you unload the dishwasher by handing you dishes to be put away.
- Put away dishes that are in lower cabinets or drawers.
- Take out the trash.
- Set and clear the table.

9- to 12-Year-Old Helpers—Jobs They Can Do

- Help write out weekly menu and shopping list.
- Assist you with grocery shopping.
- Clip coupons with supervision.
- Read recipe and retrieve items from refrigerator and pantry with supervision.
- Gather necessary bowls, measuring cups, spoons, pans, and so on.
- Measure ingredients.
- Pour ingredients into baking or stove-top pans with help and supervision.
- Turn on the oven and set the timer for cooking.
- Wipe down countertops after cooking.
- Load the dishwasher.

13- to 18-Year-Old Helpers—Jobs They Can Do

- Research the Internet for new recipe ideas.
- Create a weekly menu and shopping list.
- Teenagers who drive can complete grocery shopping on their own.
- Put away groceries.
- Help prepare foods brought home from the grocery store. For example, wash lettuce and other vegetables, make hamburger patties, cut up fruit, and so on.
- Prepare a simple meal.
- Set the table and create simple table centerpieces.

My Personal Fast-Food Kitchen Goal #10

I will choose _____ ways to include my child (children) in the preparation of _____ meals this week. And I will make a point to invite my family members into the kitchen for conversation and inclusion in the meal process.

The time you spend cultivating kitchen helpers will multiply the effectiveness of the time spent in the kitchen. Just think of how much time can be saved by delegating jobs to your children. As they grow older, you will need to spend less and less time supervising and more time working alongside your child. This is the stuff memories are made of.

Chapter 8

How to Save Money
at the Grocery Store

When I was a young mom with two preschool-aged children, one of the joys of my life was "escaping" to the grocery store. I would grab my cup of home-brewed coffee (before the invention of Starbucks) and head off to the store. For a few minutes, I could wander aimlessly through the aisles, listen to the piped-in music, sometimes sing along, and spend an hour or more browsing row after row of generously stocked shelves. I enjoyed this time spent in the grocery store. I suppose I did a lot of "window shopping" then as I roamed at a leisurely pace, but the reward for that earlier experience is that I have learned a thing or two about shopping, and I'm glad to pass it along to you.

Before my husband, Tim, became a firefighter, he was a butcher. When he worked in a retail grocery store, he began to teach me a great deal about the inner workings of the industry. One important fact stands out among the rest: Grocery stores are in the business of making money, not saving you money. I protested, "But what about sales and coupons?"

I learned early on that smart and savvy shoppers can spend less than others, but the bottom line is still the same—grocery stores don't care if you save a penny. I am speaking in general terms here, but learning this one truth will help you as you navigate through the variety of stores available to find what is best for your family's needs.

Ready, Set, Shop

In this country, we have the luxury of many different grocery store chains, each of which offer something a little different. We can shop at a small gourmet shop or the huge warehouse stores. The choices are plentiful. If you haven't explored other grocery stores in your town, I suggest that you make that a goal in the coming weeks. You might discover one that offers more of what your family likes—a wonderful produce section featuring some locally farmed goods, a butcher who will accommodate special cut requests for recipes and your family's needs, a layout that makes shopping wisely easier, and so on.

Grab your cart and let's get shopping. The following tips are divided into categories.

I encourage you to read through them a few times each week to let the ideas sink in. Ideas are great on paper, but they're more effective in action!

Plan Ahead

A little bit of time and a method of tracking what you need and when you need it will save you countless dollars and extra trips to the store. Even if you give the preparation time 10 minutes, you'll reap some big rewards in the long haul.

Try to control impulse buying. Studies have shown that almost 50% of our purchases are entirely unplanned. If you are going to allow yourself some extras, do it at the end, after your cart is full.

Make your shopping list from your meal planner. You will save approximately $25–$35 a week just by making a shopping list from your meal planner and then purchasing only what you have on the list.

Think through special events coming up. Is your son having his friends over for a campout in the backyard? Is your daughter having her soccer team over for a barbecue lunch next Saturday? If you are having houseguests for the weekend, that counts as an event when you are planning your grocery needs. And don't just think in terms of food. Do you need paper plates, paper towels, or toilet paper? My husband teaches swimming to hundreds of kids in the summer at our house! I should be a part owner in a toilet paper company by now. Plan ahead, save money, and save yourself the embarrassment of not having enough food or supplies.

TOP TEN FOODS THAT FREEZE WELL

When you are writing up that shopping list, keep these foods at the top of the list. Frozen on their own or used as ingredients for double-duty cooking, these are all winners.

1. Any ground beef or ground turkey meal
2. Chicken
3. Bacon, ham, or sausage
4. Rice
5. Cooked pancakes and waffles
6. Soups and stews
7. Cooked hamburger patties

8. Chopped onions

9. Chopped celery and bell pepper

10. Grated cheese

These foods can be stored in FoodSaver bags, sealable bags and bowls, and other plastic containers. But to get the longest life in the freezer, I highly recommend FoodSaver bags.

Coupons Mean Cash

If you think cutting coupons will take forever, consider incorporating just a few of the quick-access tips listed. You'll be surprised how simple this step can be and how much you do save. Grocery stores make money no matter what you buy. But individual companies who make and package food only make money if you buy *their* products. Why not get a deal as part of the exchange?

Use coupons. I guess I should start at the beginning. If you don't use coupons yet, give it a try. Whatever source you use for your coupons, check it, gather the ones that apply to your needs, and bring those with you. If coupons aren't part of your shopping lifestyle, read the next section of tips carefully. The effort to use coupons is worth it.

Use coupons wisely. Coupons are designed by the manufacturer to get you to buy things, not to save you money. As long as you are aware of this and are very careful about clipping and using coupons, you should be fine. Stick to your list. So what if you can get a fourth bag of potato chips if you buy three, especially when you're trying to avoid salty foods to begin with?

When cutting out coupons, mark the expiration date. Use a highlight marker and run over the expiration date. Your eye will catch it immediately. And before you get in the car to head to the grocery store, pull the ones that have expired so that you aren't disappointed at the register.

Double up when you can. If you are an avid coupon shopper, try to shop at stores where they will double the coupons. The savings will add up quickly.

Sold out doesn't mean missed out. When a store runs out of sale items, don't forget to ask for a rain check. The savings are generally substantial enough to make the effort worth it. That slip of paper will allow you the sale price when the new stock arrives, even if the sale is over.

Seek coupons through sources you are already using. If you are online a lot, check for coupons and discounts at www.coupons.com and do searches for other coupon sites. Also check with the manufacturer for specific coupons for items you use and like, such as Betty Crocker, General Mills, and others. You can even call the 1-800 phone numbers on the packaging of your favorite products. Tell them why you enjoy their product. Generally they will send coupons directly to you if you ask.

If you read the newspaper every week, start using those coupons that you used to put in the recycle bin automatically. Five minutes of paper shopping could save you plenty of money to pay for your paper subscription.

My Personal Fast-Food Kitchen Goal #11

This week I will gather several coupons from the following sources:

1.

2.

And I will take the coupons when I shop at_____.

I would love to try to save _____ dollars this month by using coupons and discounts.

Shop with Strategy

Get to know your grocery stores and how and when you shop the most efficiently. A simple goal to start with is to restrict the number of trips you make to the store. You will save a lot of money just by paying attention to your habits and setting some helpful boundaries.

Arrange your shopping list according to the floor plan of your local market. As much as possible, list foods in the order in which they are arranged in the store. This will make your trip through the market much faster and will save you from backtracking.

Complete your shopping in 30 minutes or less. Every minute you are in the store after 30 minutes, you will spend from 75 cents to 3 dollars a minute.

Get to know your store's delivery schedule. Find out which days your grocery store receives its deli, meats, and produce. Produce is usually delivered 2–3 times a week. Try to shop the day after a load is received to assure the freshest foods. If possible, shop mid-morning the day after a shipment has been received. That way, the store has had time to restock the shelves.

Make it easy on yourself. Try not to shop at 5:00 p.m. The end of the workday is the least preferred time to shop. Most people shopping at that time are in a hurry, and they're tired. To avoid lots of busy shoppers, consider shopping in the evening—8:00 p.m. or later. This also creates a more pleasurable shopping experience. You'll feel less harried, and you might even enjoy the outing.

Leave your husband and young children at home if possible. If you bring them, the potential to add items to the cart that aren't on your list greatly increases, and the distraction can cause you to miss a few items that you really needed. And never shop when you are hungry. You'll be your own distraction!

Become a Savvy Shopper

These tips will help you make better choices and become a wise shopper. Some of you might be doing these now like a pro. For any that you haven't tried, consider applying at least one to each of your future grocery outings.

Read the fine print. Compare sizes and ounces for items. Sometimes the better buy is the smaller size.

Think big, just not too big. Buy in bulk and divide into smaller packages at home. This will save you quite a bit of money. Don't, however, bulk up on items that you won't get through in a month or 6 weeks. You'll just have to deal with the storage of the items, and some items might go bad. Do keep track of those items that make sense to buy this way.

Buy what your family will actually eat. Good prices sometimes lead us to add on quantities that we wouldn't otherwise. It makes no sense to buy spaghetti sauce for a great price if no one will eat it. If you find an unbelievably low price on something your family loves, stock up. One time I found croutons (one of my husband's favorite snacks) at an unbelievable price (a third of the regular price), so I purchased 25 boxes!

Buy fruits and vegetables when in season. They will be the highest quality and the lowest price. And if you can get to a local farmers' market or shop at a store that carries some local produce, you will be getting some very healthy options for your family. Think seasonally, and you'll add flavor, variety, and nutrition to your meal plans.

Think local. You can buy locally for more than fruits and vegetables. Dairy products, breads, other baked goods, nuts, trail mixes, fresh herbs, and treats like honey are just some of the goodies you'll find at a local marketplace. You support your community, cut out the middleman, and you will get the freshest materials at a very competitive price.

Compare generic products. They generally compare quite well. Most stores will exchange an item if it doesn't meet your standards. Many times generics are processed at the same plants—they just use different labeling. Frozen vegetables are a good place to try the generic package. Remember, green beans are green beans no matter what brand the package reads.

Win savings with a "loss leader." These items are offered at a great price. As a result, you are lured into the store where the managers bank on you buying many other, more expensive items while you are there. Beat them at their own game. Each member of your family is a potential customer. Split the family up and utilize your purchasing power. Give cash to each person, and have them buy the limit of an item you use often.

Weigh your options. When buying sandwich meats, consider purchasing a whole or half ham, turkey breast, or roast beef. Then take it to the butcher, and have him slice it for you. Instead of paying from $4 to $10 a pound for prepackaged and deli meats, you will pay less than half by using this method. Split up and freeze in smaller packages once you get home. Your butcher may be willing to slice big chunks of cheese for you as well.

Set boundaries with ease. Purchase gift cards from your favorite grocery store at the beginning of each month for the budgeted amount you have to spend on groceries. When the card is empty, you know you have spent your allotted amount for that month. You can also keep track of what you have left on the card, and it will help to keep you from making unnecessary purchases.

Check that list twice. As you complete your shopping list, make sure you add extra amounts of items that you will be using for double-duty cooking, such as hamburgers, chicken breasts, pasta, and staple items including flour, sugar, broth, and more.

Plan for the emergencies. Have at least two quick emergency meals in the freezer for those unexpected crazy days—something you can simply pop in the microwave oven. You will rest easier knowing you have something on hand that can be prepared quickly.

Involve the family. Let your preteens and teenagers help you clip coupons. Make sure you only use coupons for items your family uses or for a product you would like to try. Allow your child to have the money saved on coupons. Save the rest for a nice dinner out for you and your spouse.

Teach your older preteen children to shop by asking them to seek out some of the items from the main shopping list. Teach them how to check sizes and prices for the best buy. Once they are on their own, they won't be quite as shocked that toilet paper and toothpaste aren't free!

Keep the Choices Healthy

The fast-food kitchen lifestyle depends on choices made inside and outside of the kitchen. When you drive by the exit to the restaurant and head straight home for a quick meal, or select foods that are the healthiest, or shop with a plan, you are paving the way for big changes that will greatly benefit you and your family.

Chapter 9

Your Most Important
Piece of Furniture

I don't think there is a more appealing and comforting sight than the dining room table set and ready for a meal when you walk into the house. Each family member has a special spot at the table. You might have a favorite coffee cup for Dad or child-friendly dishes for the younger children. Maybe you own a special serving dish or two. No matter what the table looks like, the message is clear—this family is loved!

Have you seen the commercial that shows different members of a family away from home, generally outside in inclement weather, closing their eyes, dreaming of hot rolls, and clicking their heels together? When they open their eyes, they are at home in front of the dining room table with a beautiful meal set before them. If you close *your* eyes, you can probably remember a special meal around the table where everything seemed perfect—no stress, no last-minute run to the grocery store or restaurant takeout counter. And each family member arrived at the same time, ready to eat.

The good feeling of a family meal isn't a fantasy. It is an attainable goal. A fast-food kitchen dinner provides a reason to come to the table and reconnect after a long day of activity.

Gathering at the Table

On a typical day for a busy mom, the family has been gone since morning. And people have made few exchanges since, except maybe a phone call or a text message. When everyone goes their separate way after they say good morning, the family suffers a physical disconnect from one another. Even if you keep each other in your thoughts and prayers during the day to maintain an emotional connection, the physical distance creates a separation. It becomes necessary, then, to find a way to bridge that gap of different experiences, priorities, and concerns each time you are together. Now dinner becomes more than just food—it becomes the chance for members of the family unit to reunite and discuss the day's happenings with joy and laughter. The dinner table takes on a role of great importance.

When you return to the tradition of a shared meal, you realize how vital this time is for the health of the family. It doesn't matter what's on the table. The most important ingredients are right there—conversation, laughter, storytelling, devoted attention, and care. Everyone is on the same page once again. And for the mom who manages the details for this event to take place, this is a time of rich assurance and satisfaction.

Since the kitchen is the heart of the home, the dining room table becomes the hub of action. Many things occur at that table beyond eating. Relationships are developing between husband and wife, parents and children, and welcome guests—friends, extended family, and neighbors. Several years ago, our pastor encouraged us to "learn to barbecue first." He was trying to teach us that as we reach out to neighbors and friends with a warm meal and building friendships, it becomes much easier to show them the Jesus we love. Sometimes we socialize and play a few games. When the conversation turns to spiritual things, we have set the tone for a relationship, and they will want to listen. There is no need to hit them over the head with the Bible. Instead, we just live the Bible!

We had a wonderful experience that lasted over a couple of years, and it really illustrates this point. I had a home-based word-processing business that allowed me to meet many wonderful people as they came to me for typing work. One was a very sweet man named David. He worked long hours in Riverside, where we lived, but his home was 60 miles away in Los Angeles. Because of his long hours and heavy workload (and the heavy traffic in this part of California), David would stay in a very small one-room apartment during the week and go home on the weekends. Since his computer skills were not as sharp as he would have liked, he became a regular customer of my word-processing business.

When he stopped by with work for me, he always brought something extra—a delicious baked delicacy for my family. Often we would have him join us for dinner. David had grown up in war-torn Germany during World War II. The life he lived as a Jewish man during the Holocaust was something completely unfathomable to my family. The stories he shared with our family around our dining room table will never be forgotten. Living in the comfort of this amazing country, we had a difficult time imagining what he had endured. We had an opportunity to experience living history with this very soft-spoken and kind man. We were able to pray with him and be loving and kind. We let him see Jesus in our family.

What Can Bring Your Family to the Table

If your family rarely gathers at the dining room table for anything other than a couple of dinners each week at best, it is time to find more reasons to come to the table. Make the opportunities inviting, fun, and a chance for casual conversations and even some meaningful dialogue. It all happens when families big or small gather at the table. It also happens when you welcome old friends, neighbors, and new friends to this place of hospitality. Explore these ideas and adopt a few for your personal plan of action. Your family—and others—will thank you.

1. *Breakfast time.* Starting the day around the table can be a wonderful tradition that sets you and your family out into the world on the right foot. It becomes the chance to look each family member in the eyes and smile. Let them know they are special and loved. Breakfast time is the *real family*. Some family breakfast tables are lively with conversation about the day's happenings or reminders of appointments and things that are not to be forgotten. And there are some breakfast tables where few words are spoken. Valuing one another even in the quiet and still is part of what makes family so unique and important. No matter how simple the meal, the time you spend together is about developing relationships—a discussion of a child's dream and what it means, prayers for an upcoming test, or encouraging words to your husband and children before they are off for the rest of the day.

   We set the tone in the home. It is so important to realize that not only *what* we say but also *how we say it* makes a difference in the lives of those we live with. What happens in the morning sets the tone for the whole day. The day is not in motion. A simple breakfast, smiles, and a hug go a long way to developing self-worth in our family. And Mom, it gives you a chance to oversee what the day holds for your troops. Even if you are out the door to work, you are still the glue that holds the family together. You give the sense of security and well-being. It's a big job, but the rewards are worth it. That big hug and kiss before they leave makes our day pretty wonderful as well.

2. *Game night.* Another great function of the dining room table is a place to gather and play games. Some of our favorite memories are at the dining room table deeply involved in a game of Chutes and Ladders, Go Fish, Hearts, Pictionary, Scrabble, Phase 10, or Monopoly. Playing games is good for the family because it teaches skills, fairness, and teamwork. And I guarantee you this: If you have more than one child, you will also discover that you will have at least one cheater! The competition of playing and winning is more than some children can handle. So game night can also become a teaching opportunity as we guide our children to be gracious losers and winners!

3. *Homework and school projects.* Assigned homework and school projects need to be worked on where you can inspect what is being done. The dining room table is a great place to make that happen. It keeps your child on task and keeps you available for questions and guidance. I highly suggest a "family computer" near the dining room table for easy access and supervision. There is a less likely chance of game playing or exploration if the computer is in clear view of Mom or Dad instead of in a child's room.

And remember, a plate of cookies, a cup of milk, and a hug can be a great encouragement for difficult math problems!

4. *Coffee or tea with a neighbor.* I love to visit with my neighbors over a cup of coffee or tea. My neighbors know that if my kitchen Dutch door is open, they are free to drop by. A kind word, sweet conversation, and a prayer can go a long way in the lives of our friends. And don't forget your family. Your spouse or child will appreciate some one-on-one time over a warm cup of comfort.

5. *Bible study.* This is my time for Bible study, prayer, journaling, and reading. I enjoy my early morning coffee as I read and study. It is a cozy and relaxing time to sit and ponder, wonder, and dream. Show your family that this is a place for this kind of commitment and peaceful rest.

6. *Family devotions.* If you have family devotions or have considered starting them, I highly recommend using the dining room table as the place to gather. As you read and study the Bible, you have a place to work and write. It emphasizes the importance of the family unit and the family's faith.

7. *Talking to God.* My husband, Tim, loves the dining room table and considers it a very special place. He will tell you the dining room table is where he learned to pray out loud. Tim was not raised in the church and had little experience with praying out loud around others. During our meal times, sitting around the table, he would pray beautiful and simple prayers over our food. The more often he prayed, the more comfortable he became with praying. Because of that starting place at the table, he now enjoys the opportunity to pray in a group setting, both small and large. You can teach your children to pray around the dining room table. Some of the sweetest prayers have occurred around our table during a meal.

8. *Crafts and creativity.* The dining room table can be a great place to let your children explore their creative and artistic side. You can make it a place to draw, paint, build, create, and write. It becomes yet another way to instill the importance of spending time around the table. Provide the necessary tools and let your children loose to discover their hidden talents. You might find you have the next Rembrandt or C.S. Lewis.

9. *Lessons in manners and kindness.* As families sit down to a meal, the dining room table becomes a teaching table. Moms and dads spend hours teaching table manners and how one is supposed to behave at the table. The repetition of teaching over and over is how you get the job done.

My Personal Fast-Food Kitchen Goal #12

I am excited to use the dining room table to welcome a sense of community and connection into my home. I will use the table in these three ways to start new table traditions with my family and/or friends:

1.

2.

3.

Other family happenings make the dining room table vital to the health and well-being of your family. The list is endless, and your list would be different from mine, but this indicates the importance of what happens when time is spent together as a family.

There is a special power at the dining room table. Don't clutter your table with piles of paper and stuff that doesn't have a home. Resist using it for storage. File it, put it away, or throw it out. The table needs to stay cleared off. Make your dining table the center of activity for your home. Use it often. Sometimes when I pass by the dining room table, I pause for a moment. I can almost see Tim and the kids enjoying a meal or playing a game. And I'm sure I hear the laughter and fun. It's a treasured memory I will never forget.

Chapter 10

Fast-Food with Friends

There was a time, not too many years ago, when entertaining centered mostly around the home. Friends dropped by for coffee and cake, or they might visit for a Sunday afternoon lunch. Entertaining involved gathering around the dinner table or out in the backyard for a barbecue. Meals were simple and delicious—enjoyed at a leisurely pace along with pleasant conversation.

Fast-forward to today, and statistics state that more than 80 percent of entertaining is now done in restaurants. I believe there is a time and a place for restaurant entertaining, but we need to rediscover the joy of hospitality and entertaining at home. Most of us don't entertain any longer at home because we have unbelievable schedules and are pulled in so many different directions. Our daily pace keeps us stressed, overworked, and overtired. The thought of entertaining at home is the furthest from our minds. That pace also means that our homes are often cluttered, and the idea of preparing our living spaces for public viewing is overwhelming. And more than a few of us have bought into the idea that entertaining is something that other people do well, but not us.

But hospitality can be easy and fun, as long as we keep it simple. One dictionary defines *hospitality* as "the friendly reception and treatment of guests or strangers" and "the quality or disposition of receiving and treating guests and strangers in a warm, friendly, generous way."

What beautiful definitions of a beautiful word. But for many, the word *hospitality* strikes fear down deep in their hearts. Hospitality is not about where you live, your decorating style, what furniture you have, the dishes you own, or what food will be served. It is the spirit of hospitality that is desired. It is a sense of warmth and welcome that is evident the minute you open the front door and greet your guests!

Hospitality can be well planned, or it can be a spur-of-the-moment event. Spontaneous hospitality is my favorite kind of entertaining. In that case, I don't have time to get stressed, and the expectations of my guests are within reach. Some of the best moments we have shared with others have been impromptu, last-minute decisions to open our hearts and home. You don't even have to have a meal. Just a quick cup of coffee, a piece of pie, and some wonderful conversation.

You might be thinking, *Well, I just don't have the time or money!* In reality, it doesn't have to cost much, and the time investment will be worth the outcome. It mostly takes a willing heart. Everything else naturally falls into place.

Fast-Food Kitchen Entertaining

The secret you will uncover is that once you embrace the fast-food kitchen ideas, you begin to think differently about serving others, building community, and nurturing yourself, your family, and others. You discover that instead of fretting about meals or doing everything perfectly, you actually have the gift of joy. You can savor the moments of being with your family or with guests who enter your home. Even unexpected guests become opportunities to shower people with hospitality.

It is very freeing to let go of the worry and to step into your kitchen with confidence and delight. The fast-food methods will help you graciously prepare and present your meal, whether it's a big casserole, a seven-course meal, or a game day buffet of chips, salsa, and tacos.

Here are some helpful tips and doses of encouragement to turn your fast-food kitchen lifestyle into one that includes carefree hospitality.

Don't set your expectations too high. Start small and grow from there. Use your family and close friends as your "guinea pigs" until you get really confident in your entertaining finesse.

Keep it simple! Everyone loves simplicity. The simpler your entertaining is from the meal to the table setting, the less stressed you will feel, and you will truly be able to enjoy yourself and your guests.

Consider including others in the planning. Always ask for help. People genuinely love to help, and this becomes an opportunity for more fellowship, conversation, and a sense of belonging for your kids and guests. If you are serving buffet style, have one person assigned to each dish to oversee the last touches and to set it up on the counter or table for serving. Just finishing the cupcakes? Perfect. In fact, plan the timing this way to make the gathering fun. Give the kids or even your adult guests the task of frosting the cupcakes. This brings out the joy in people of all ages. Have lots of spoons for people to lick!

Don't spend unnecessary money. Sure enough, when your party is two days away, you'll start wishing you had a bigger table, more comfortable couch, larger serving platter, or more festive decorations. Don't go on a shopping spree that you'll regret. Absorb this lesson now, right away: You don't need to buy everything, own everything, and do everything. Don't be shy—ask for help and delegate tasks such as cleaning, setting the table, and picking out games. Instead of buying, borrow anything you can. This includes dishes, centerpieces, extra tables, chairs, and more.

Think differently about what a home event looks like. Don't go the way of fancy if that is not what would appeal to your guests or suit everyone's busy schedules. And don't feel as though you are in charge of all the food. Potlucks are great ways to entertain without the stress of planning and preparing the entire meal. Offer to serve the main meats or entrée and some basic beverages, and then let others bring side dishes like salad, veggies, mashed potatoes, appetizers, and even desserts.

Think outside the box...or with the box! To set up a unique serving table for a buffet, find several different-sized, sturdy cardboard boxes and place them on the table at different angles. You might even consider stacking a few of them in the center. Place a large tablecloth or king-size flat sheet to cover the boxes. Place the serving dishes on top of each of the flat areas of the boxes and around the outside flat part of the table. It looks like a fancy buffet table that is easy to assemble and easy to take apart at the end of the evening.

Go with what works. Don't try to use a new recipe for entertaining. Serve meals that have stood the test of time with your family and close friends. It is very tempting to start expanding your repertoire of recipes a week before your gathering. But that will only add stress to your day. Believe me. So instead of adding new recipes that might go badly, add extra special touches to what is a proven dish. Drizzle pesto on the chicken breasts. Add chives to your ranch dip. Shape a centerpiece out of fresh herbs. Those extra touches become the really fun part of entertaining. Bag ice cubes in brown paper lunch sacks. The cubes won't stick, and you will have plenty for dinner parties and get-togethers. Also great for extra summertime needs.

My Personal Fast-Food Kitchen Goal #13

I will let go of my preconceived ideas about what entertaining involves. I will make my home welcoming and will plan to have people over _____ times this month in order to extend the fast-food kitchen lifestyle to acts of hospitality.

Fast-Food Kitchen Tips for Indoor Entertaining

1. One week before your event, make a simple to-do list and a separate menu. For a more budget-friendly event, consider a buffet: You provide the main dish, and others bring the side dishes and desserts.

2. Delegate as much as possible—setting the table, pulling out serving dishes, cleaning, and so on.

3. Two days ahead, prepare any dishes that can be assembled ahead of time and cooked the day of your party. This includes salads and desserts.

4. If a recipe must be assembled and cooked the day of your party, you can still chop vegetables or measure dry ingredients for a recipe ahead of time. Dry seasonings can be placed in small food-safe bowls and placed in the refrigerator. Cheese can be grated and stored in a food-safe bowl or bag.

5. Set your table the day before your party. This allows you to make sure you have everything you need and gives you the opportunity to experiment and change things around once you have everything out. It saves so much time if you don't have to set the table the day of your get-together. Prepare a simple centerpiece. Place seasonal fruits and vegetables down the middle of the table with votive candles. Note: When using candles on the table, make sure they have no scent to interfere with the smells of your food.

6. The day of your party, make sure you have plenty of ice for drinks. Set up the coffee pot ahead of time—preferably 2–3 hours before guests arrive. Have an additional filter with coffee already measured out in case you have a lot of coffee drinkers. If your party is in the evening, make sure to offer decaffeinated coffee as well as regular. Consider hot tea as an option as well.

7. Spend a few minutes tidying up, making sure to double-check the guest bathroom.

8. Allow plenty of time for you to shower and dress so you will be fresh as a flower as your guests arrive.

9. Light candles a half hour before your guests are due to arrive. Candles say "Welcome!"

Fast-Food Kitchen Tips for Outdoor Entertaining

1. Check weather forecasts and plan accordingly. If you live where there are uncertain weather patterns, have a backup plan in place for less welcoming weather changes.

2. If hosting a barbecue, season and freeze hamburger patties 2 days before. If serving chicken or ribs, begin marinating the day before.

3. Make your pasta, potato salads, and any desserts 2 days ahead of time.

4. Begin making and saving extra ice. Store it in brown lunch sacks. It won't stick together and stays fresh.

5. Clean up patio furniture and hose down the patio area 1 day ahead of time for a clean, fresh look.

6. Set out dishes you will use. Consider paper plates to keep cleanup to a minimum.

7. The day of your party, set the table early. Cut up veggies and fruit. Make iced tea or lemonade and ice down the drinks. Now you can rest and relax and enjoy your guests.

Dream Up a Theme

When you aren't overly worried about the food aspect of a gathering, you are free to explore more ways to make an evening or afternoon with friends more enjoyable and entertaining. Many of the ideas listed here can also make for a fun family night. Don't limit your heart for hospitality just to guests.

- *"Come as you are" party.* This is especially fun to do with neighbors or very close friends. Call everyone and tell them to come on over wearing whatever they have on at that moment! Have everyone grab a snack from the refrigerator or pantry to share. Have the camera ready for some great "Kodak" moments. Sometimes the impromptu gatherings are the ones that most people can attend.

- *Progressive dinner.* This is a great way to get together with several different friends at one another's homes. You need one home for each course: hors d'oeuvres, soup, salad, main dish, and dessert. This is great for neighborhood families or small groups of friends. You can keep the number of couples to how many courses you will serve, or you can have host homes and make the group larger.

- *Supper six or supper eight night.* This idea is for groups of three or four couples at one time. Once a month for three or four months, assign a different couple in the group to host the meal in their home. Rotate homes, and you can start over at the end with a new group of couples. This works great for churches, clubs, or neighborhoods.

- *Backyard barbecues.* Invite friends, extended family, and neighbors. Barbecue and play games. Keep it simple and economic by using paper goods and having each guest family bring a dish or their own meat for the grill. By dining outside, you keep the mess and cleanup to a minimum. And people expect a barbeque to be casual and "go with the flow," which allows you to wing it and enjoy it a bit more than a sit-down dinner.

- *Swim and sundaes.* Host a summertime pool party. Serve iced tea or lemonade. Make homemade ice cream or build your own ice cream sundae bar.

- *Hors d'oeuvres recipe exchange.* Invite friends to come over and bring their favorite hors d'oeuvres along with a copy of the recipe for each person. An evening of appetizers and great conversation is so enjoyable, and the advance preparation is next to nothing. And you will each come away with some useful recipes for future gatherings.

- *Game night.* Invite friends over for a simple meal and game night. Board games, card games, and bunco are big hits. If you don't want to have a full meal, simply serve snacks and/or dessert. Have small fun prizes for the winners!

  Game night can also be about a professional sports event. For your friends who enjoy watching sports on television, plan a party for the big game. Encourage everyone to wear team colors. Finger foods are best for game day.

- *Awards show night.* Host an awards dinner party or buffet. There are many to choose from—Academy Awards, Grammy Awards, People's Choice Awards, and so forth. Everyone roots for their favorite actors or singers. Have score sheets where each person can choose who they think will win for the top 4–5 categories. Have a mock statue for the winner who gets the most right.

- *Reality show extravaganza.* Normally, gathering friends just to watch television isn't too conducive to community or conversation. But with the rise of reality shows' popularity, most of us have friends who are mutual fans of a show or two…and there is fun to be had! *Survivor, The Amazing Race,* and *American Idol* are only a few of the reality shows that make for great group entertainment. You can get together weekly and watch the show's progress. Keep snacks and decorating simple. Have each person bring something, or pitch in for a pizza. For the show's finale, have a special evening where folks guess, in advance, who the winner will be. Invite each family or individual to make a small donation toward the purchase of fun prizes to be awarded to the winner(s).

These are just a few ideas to help you create your own personal entertaining ideas. Once you start entertaining at home again, you'll be hooked. Entertaining deepens friendships and opens the door to new friendships as you open your heart and your home.

Chapter 11

Traditions to Nurture Family Togetherness

Lazy Saturday morning country breakfasts, Sunday afternoon pot roasts at Nana's house, family pasta nights with generous portions served in the special spaghetti bowl, breezy fall picnics under the trees drinking hot chocolate, and coffee from a thermos while munching on the best oatmeal cookies ever made. These are sweet memories for me. What are your delicious recollections of food and family times?

Family traditions and memories are important as they are being created, and they are important as they leave a legacy of nurturing and nourishment to be passed down from generation to generation. Many years ago, I read a profound quote from Dr. James Dobson that I will paraphrase for you here: If you want your children to return home for more than just obligatory visits after they are grown, you must have established family traditions and memories.

Each family is unique, and our personalized traditions reveal this and also nurture a sense of unity and belonging. Webster defines *tradition* as "the handing down of information, beliefs, and customs by word of mouth or by example from one generation to another without written instruction."

Traditions and family rituals, especially those around the table, are vital to the health of our families. They are shaped when we come together for a time of laughing, sharing, playing, eating, and just having fun. Establishing traditions in stepfamilies today is vitally important for the new family to succeed. Blending old traditions with the new ones can help ensure success.

Sometimes traditions occur with deliberate intention, and other times they are born out of a situation quite by accident. No matter how a tradition is established, it can set the tone for your particular family. Traditions make your family stand out among all the other families around. Many of the best traditions start in the kitchen and around the dining room table. I encourage you to look at the ideas below and use your creativity and imagination to make them unique for your particular family.

1. *Birthday parties.* When I was a child, birthday parties were always held at home. There really were no other options. You played a few games, opened

presents, and ate homemade cake and ice cream. Simple, easy, and fun. When my children were growing up, parties moved out of the home and to McDonald's, the skating rink, the bowling alley, and other places. But the parties my children remember most were the parties we held at home. You can be as creative as you like and add to the festivities as your budget allows. Use the Internet to get ideas for themes, favors, and recipes.

- Consider a sleepover for girls.
- Boys typically enjoy camping out in the backyard (weather permitting).
- You might hold parties at a nearby park.
- Pool parties make great celebrations for summer birthdays.
- When hosting a sleepover party, arrange a neighborhood scavenger hunt or a late-night run to the yogurt shop.
- What about a "progressive birthday party"? Start the party at a friend's home with snacks and a game. Move to a second home (Grandma's or another friend's place) for homemade pizza, soda, and another game. The last stop is back at your home where you open presents and have cake and ice cream.
- Don't forget to videotape the fun and festivities for a fun family movie night later on!

2. *Outdoor barbecues and picnics.* Two of the things I like most about summer are the long days and opportunities to dine outside. Backyard barbecues are such fun, and they provide many opportunities for making family memories. You can spread out a blanket and dine out in the yard under a shade tree. Consider a water balloon or water gun fight. Team up family members and have fun. Go out for ice cream sundaes after you clean up.

   You can pack a few things and get on the open road to savor outdoor fun with new scenery. Prepare a picnic lunch with cold goodies from your double-duty cooking favorites and go to the park, the mountains, or the beach. It's a great way to relax and enjoy the sunshine. Don't forget a Frisbee, football, or kite.

3. *Gatherings to practice hospitality.* It is important to teach your children the gift of hospitality—entertaining friends and extended family. It doesn't come naturally to everyone, so teaching the art of entertaining will be quite beneficial as your children grow up and start homes and families of their own. By hosting simple get-togethers, your children will learn a great deal. In the Bible, we are commanded to extend lodging and meals to strangers.

By demonstrating the art of hospitality, we are setting a great example for our children. Does your child of dating age have a boyfriend or girlfriend? Invite that special person to a family dinner. It's a great way to get to know the person your teenager spends time with. Sharing a meal together allows you to see what your child sees. It also gives you a chance to ask questions and listen to find out the heart of the person who is dating your son or daughter.

4. *Tea parties or fireplace picnics with your kids.* One of the greatest ways to connect with your children, stepchildren, or grandchildren is to spend time in meaningful communication.

    I found that the best way for me to connect to my daughter was while having tea. I started tea parties with Terra when she was only eight. They were always simple. It doesn't matter what you serve to drink or eat. It is the spirit of the tea party that matters.

    Most of our tea parties were early in the morning before school. I would set up the tea table and call her to join me. We had each other's undivided attention for just a few minutes. She would share her heart, and I could listen and learn. We would have tea parties the first day of school, the last day of school, her birthday, my birthday, and anytime we were having difficulty connecting. No matter what was going on in her life, she always loved taking time for a tea party with Mom.

    If you have boys, you can offer the same kind of activity with a bit of a rustic spirit. Spread out a quilt in front of the fireplace and serve mugs of hot chocolate. The most important thing to offer them is a listening ear and a chance to connect.

5. *Serve family favorites.* At least once a week, try serving one of your entire family's favorite meals. Real comfort foods create some of the most cherished traditions. Make sure it is on a night when everyone will be home. During dinner, take turns sharing a favorite family memory. The laughter and fun will be unforgettable.

6. *Extended family gatherings.* We're in a time when families no longer seem to gather for weekly Sunday dinners, and keeping family togetherness takes determination. Try to include extended family—grandparents, aunts, uncles, or cousins—in a meal every few weeks. It's fun to reconnect and find out what is going on in the lives of those you call family. It can be for a barbecue or pie and coffee. Making the effort will be worth it.

7. *Holiday meals and traditions.* The word *holidays* conjures up wonderful memories of days gone by and fun shared with family and friends. It seems that when the holiday season rolls around, we take a walk back in time.

Many holiday traditions center around food. Growing up, our entire family and relatives would spend the Thanksgiving holiday at Joshua Tree National Park in the high desert of Southern California. It was a magical place. We would take my grandparents' trailer out to the high desert, and Nana would cook an entire turkey dinner in that small trailer kitchen. We would hike, play, and eat all day long. As the day wound down, it was time to sit around the campfire, drink coffee, eat dessert, and share stories about the fun of the day.

What holiday memories do you hold dear? What did you always want to do for the holidays but never got to? Let the answers to these questions spark the creation of lasting, family activities that will help your children feel connected. For Christmas, the simplest events might be the most meaningful—heading to the woods or lot to pick the best Christmas tree, attending a Christmas Eve service, caroling with the neighbors, and having eggnog and pancakes while opening presents. Don't forget Memorial Day, the Fourth of July, and birthdays. Make the most of every occasion.

8. *"You are special today."* Rejoice as a family and sing the praises of one of your kids or your spouse in a clever way. All it takes is a special plate tucked in your cupboard and brought out to celebrate milestones in the family—birthdays, good report cards, promotions, achievements, and other such things. We use a bright red plate. There's never a doubt who the person of honor is when that red plate is on the table.

    As an extra treat, make that person's favorite meal or dessert. Take time to have each person seated at the table share what is special about the red plate recipient. When guests come for dinner, consider honoring them with the plate you use for this fun tradition. You can even take pictures of the plate honoree.

9. *Giving as a tradition.* Teaching children compassion is best done by example. Once in a while, make a dinner to take to someone elderly who lives alone. It could be a neighbor or someone from your church. Or surprise a busy mom of young children with a homemade casserole.

10. *Serve an "opposite meal."* A fun tradition is to change up dinner by serving dessert first. Your kids will really enjoy this. If you do this once every month or so, take turns choosing the special dessert that starts off the meal.

11. *First-day-of-school special lunch.* Create a special tradition of making a very special first-day-of-school lunch for your children—complete with things they won't normally find in their bags. I also include a love note.

12. *Movie night.* This is a great time for the family. Choose a movie early in the

week so they have something to look forward to. Make bowls of popcorn, and have soda and candy ready for "intermission." Tim always had fun with this. He would set up a couple rows of chairs "theater style" in the living room, turn off all the lights, and use a flashlight to keep the noise down.

13. *Make a funny family video.* Technology has made recording fun events so easy. Regularly record your children doing silly and funny things. Encourage your kids to sing and dance for the camera. Record your kids learning to ride a bike or roller skate. The memories will be precious, and you will have something to hold over their heads as they begin dating. See, it can be fun to think ahead too. The movies become great fun to watch as a family as the kids grow older. They love seeing themselves when they were young.

My Personal Fast-Food Kitchen Goal #14

My family needs traditions that nurture them. I will build up this one tradition that we already do: _____. I'd like to try the following ideas to shape two new simple traditions in the coming months:

1.

2.

Traditions have an important place in the family. Taking time to establish ones that involve the entire family will draw you together. Recognize the importance of traditions, even the silly ones. Kids will learn to count on them and will draw a deep sense of love, confidence, creativity, and the value of family from these times. Get everyone on board helping. There is great pleasure in living, laughing, playing, and loving your family!

My Personal Fast-Food
Kitchen Goals Master Page

A s you fill in these personal goals within the text of the chapters, also fill in your answers on this master page. Keep this for quick reference and for encouragement along the way.

My Personal Fast-Food Kitchen Goal #1

During this next month, I will place value on my family's health by doing the first item on the healthy changes list. I will also choose a healthier life by doing the following four others from the list: #_____, #_____, #_____, and #_____.

My Personal Fast-Food Kitchen Goal #2

I will be willing to take baby steps now and in the following weeks. My goal is to make the following three changes to the way I approach food, cooking for my family, and my kitchen:

1.

2.

3.

My Personal Fast-Food Kitchen Goal #3

I will change the way I view eating out. I will save eating at _____ restaurant for the following upcoming occasion or celebration: _____.

My Personal Fast-Food Kitchen Goal #4

I will create an efficient, pleasant space by taking simple steps and spending ____ minutes a day for ____ weeks to shape my personalized fast-food kitchen.

My Personal Fast-Food Kitchen Goal #5

I will clear out the clutter and the unnecessary items in my kitchen, including the following items:

And I will make room for a more efficient way of cooking, eating, and living.

My Personal Fast-Food Kitchen Goal #6

I will review the pantry basics list and will create my personal version by_____ (date). And I will plan to buy a few items each _____ until my pantry is well stocked and suits the most frequent needs of my family. These are the items I know I want to get right away:

1.   4.

2.   5.

3.   6.

My Personal Fast-Food Kitchen Goal #7

I will start practicing double-duty cooking _____ times a week for this first month. I will keep it simple so that it is not stressful, and I will strive to make it a new way of viewing and using time in the kitchen.

My Personal Fast-Food Kitchen Goal #8

This week I will select _____ favorite recipes and write them out on three-by-five cards, or I will use another system that works best with my resources and preferences. These are the three that come to my mind right away:

1.

2.

3.

My Personal Fast-Food Kitchen Goal #9

I will try to add _____ recipes a month to my favorites file.

My Personal Fast-Food Kitchen Goal # 10

I will choose _____ ways to include my child (children) in the preparation of _____ meals this week. And I will make a point to invite my family members into the kitchen for conversation and inclusion in the meal process.

My Personal Fast-Food Kitchen Goal #11

This week I will gather several coupons from the following sources:

1.

2.

And I will take the coupons when I shop at _____.

I would love to try to save _____ dollars this month by using coupons and discounts.

My Personal Fast-Food Kitchen Goal #12

I am excited to use the dining room table to welcome a sense of community and connection into my home. I will use the table in these three ways to start new table traditions with my family and/or friends:

1.

2.

3.

My Personal Fast-Food Kitchen Goal #13

I will let go of my preconceived ideas about what entertaining involves. I will make my home welcoming and will plan to have people over _____ times this month in order to extend the fast-food kitchen lifestyle to acts of hospitality.

My Personal Fast-Food Kitchen Goal #14

My family needs traditions that nurture them. I will build up this one tradition that we already do:_____. I'd like to try the following ideas to shape two new simple traditions in the coming months:

1.

2.

More than 100 Fast-Food Kitchen Recipes

Breakfast

Main Dishes

Veggies, Sides, and Salads

Desserts

Breakfast

❧ Alaskan Blueberry Coffee Cake ❧

Prep Time: 20 minutes

Total Cooking Time: 25–30 minutes

Fast-Food Meal Prep Time: 15 minutes

Serves: 8

Approximate Calories per Serving: 425

Ingredients

1½ cups all-purpose flour

¾ cup granulated sugar

2½ tsp. baking powder

1 tsp. salt

¼ cup vegetable oil

¾ cup milk

1 large egg

1½ cups fresh blueberries, divided

Topping

⅓ cup all-purpose flour

½ cup brown sugar, firmly packed

½ tsp. ground cinnamon

¼ cup butter

Method

Preheat oven to 375°. Grease a 9 x 9-inch square pan; set aside.

In a medium-sized mixing bowl, blend together 1½ cups flour, sugar, baking powder, salt, oil, milk, egg, and 1 cup blueberries. Beat thoroughly for 30 seconds and spread into prepared pan.

In a medium mixing bowl, combine topping ingredients and mix until crumbly. Sprinkle mixture evenly over batter and top with the remaining ½ cup berries.

Bake for 25–30 minutes or until tested done when wooden pick inserted in center comes out clean. Do not overbake. Cool slightly. Serve warm.

Tools Needed

9 x 9-inch casserole pan

Medium mixing bowl

Large spoon

Measuring cups

Measuring spoons

Side Dishes

Serve with scrambled eggs and bacon, ham, or sausage.

Fast-Food Kitchen Tip

❧ Use premeasured dry ingredients for the batter and topping.

Double-Duty Cooking Tip

❧ When measuring dry ingredients for the batter and topping, make two extra servings and place in an airtight container. Store in the refrigerator or pantry for use in this recipe later in the month. Don't forget to mark the container!

❧ Bread and Butter Breakfast Casserole ❧

By Mary Amiot

Prep Time: 15 minutes

Total Cooking Time: 65 minutes

Fast-Food Meal Prep Time: 7–10 minutes

Serves: 8 generously

Approximate Calories per Serving: 475

Ingredients

1 lb. Jimmy Dean Sausage (hot)

1 lb. Jimmy Dean Sausage (regular or lite)

1 loaf white bread

¼ lb. butter, softened

2 cups shredded cheddar cheese

2 cups shredded Monterey Jack cheese

8 eggs

3 cups milk

1 tsp. salt

½ tsp. garlic powder

½ tsp. Dijon mustard

2 cans (4 oz. each) diced green chilies

Method

Butter one side of the bread and layer the bottom of a 9 x 13-inch pan, butter side down. Sprinkle half the cheese and uncooked, crumbled sausage on the bread. Repeat with a second layer.

In a medium-sized mixing bowl, combine the eggs, milk, salt, garlic powder, mustard, and chilies. Mix well and pour over the bread, cheese, and sausage layers. Chill 24 hours in the refrigerator. Bake at 325° for 65 minutes.

Tools Needed

9 x 13-inch casserole pan

Medium-sized mixing bowl

Large spoon

Can opener

Measuring cups

Measuring spoons

Side Dishes

Fresh fruit

Fast-Food Kitchen Tip

⇥ Use preshredded cheese.

⇥ Thaw frozen casserole and reheat in oven until warm through, approximately 30 minutes.

Double-Duty Cooking Tip

⇥ Make two 8 x 8-inch casseroles instead of one 9 x 13-inch casserole. Cook both casseroles and freeze one for a meal later in the week or month.

⇥ Double the recipe and cook two 9 x 13-inch casseroles. Freeze one large casserole for a meal later in the month.

Cheesy Scrambled Eggs

Prep Time: 15 minutes

Total Cooking Time: 7–10 minutes

Fast-Food Meal Prep Time: 10 minutes

Serves: 4

Approximate Calories per Serving: 425

Ingredients

⅓ cup cream cheese, softened

2 T. half-and-half

8 large eggs

⅓ cup grated Parmesan cheese

½ tsp. pepper

⅛ tsp. salt

6–8 slices bacon, cooked and crumbled
(can use ½ cup diced, cooked ham)

2 T. butter

Method

In a medium mixing bowl, whisk together the cream cheese and half-and-half until smooth. Add the eggs, Parmesan cheese, salt, and pepper and stir until mixed well. Add the bacon (or ham). Heat butter in a skillet and add egg mixture. Cook over a low to medium heat, stirring constantly until set. Serve immediately.

Tools Needed

Skillet

Medium mixing bowl

Whisk

Measuring cups

Measuring spoons

Side Dishes

Toast or biscuits

Fresh fruit

Fast-Food Kitchen Tip

↠ Use preshredded cheese.

↠ Use precrumbled or cubed bacon or ham.

↠ Prepare mixture before bed the night before and store in an airtight container in the refrigerator.

Double-Duty Cooking Tip

↠ When shredding Parmesan cheese, shred extra and store in a FoodSaver bag in the freezer.

↠ Cook extra bacon, crumble and store in a FoodSaver bag and freeze.

↠ Cube extra ham and store in a FoodSaver bag and freeze.

Chocolate-Chip Cinnamon Breakfast Ring

By Melinda Allison

Prep Time: 15 minutes

Total Cooking Time: 25 minutes

Fast-Food Meal Prep Time: 10 minutes

Serves: 8–10 generously

Approximate Calories per Serving: 350

Ingredients

½ cup butter, melted

3 cans (12.4 oz. each) cinnamon rolls with icing (Pillsbury brand works best), quartered

1 pkg. (3.4 oz.) vanilla pudding (just the powder—NOT instant)

½ cup brown sugar

¾ cup mini chocolate chips

Method

Grease a Bundt pan and layer the quartered cinnamon rolls, pudding powder, brown sugar, and chocolate chips. Make three layers. Then pour the melted butter evenly over the top. Bake at 375° for 24–28 minutes. Pour slightly warmed icing (included in the cinnamon roll packages) over the baked ring. Serve warm.

Tools Needed

Bundt pan

Measuring cups

Small bowl

Kitchen scissors

Side Dishes

Fresh fruit

Scrambled eggs

Bacon, ham, or sausage

Fast-Food Kitchen Tip

⊸ Use premeasured dry ingredients (pudding, brown sugar, and chocolate chips).

Double-Duty Cooking Tip

⊸ When making this recipe, measure an extra mixture of the pudding, brown sugar, and chocolate chips and place in a food-safe container with tight-fitting lid. Store in the refrigerator or freezer for use the next time you make the breakfast ring.

☃ Christmas Breakfast Casserole ☃

Prep Time: 15 minutes
Total Cooking Time: 50 minutes
Fast-Food Meal Prep Time: 10 minutes

Serves: 6–8 generously
Approximate Calories per Serving: 375

Ingredients
1 bag frozen, shredded hash browns
Salt and pepper to taste
4 T. butter, melted
1 cup fully cooked ham, cubed (you can also
use bacon or sausage or a combination
of all three—cooked and chopped or
crumbled)
8 eggs
¼ cup milk
1 cup shredded cheddar cheese

Method
Layer shredded frozen hash browns in a
9 x 13-inch pan, sprayed lightly with cooking
spray. Salt and pepper to taste and then pour
butter evenly over the top. (*This can be done
ahead of time; cover the pan and place in the
refrigerator until time to continue.*) Bake hash
browns in the oven at 350° for 20 minutes or
until tender. Remove from the oven and top
evenly with meat. Whisk eggs with milk and
pour over the hash browns and meat mixture.
Sprinkle cheese on the top and return to the
oven for another 20–30 minutes.

Tools Needed
9 x 13-inch casserole pan
Mixing bowl
Whisk
Measuring cups
Measuring spoons
Paring knife

Side Dishes
Fresh fruit
Biscuits

Fast-Food Kitchen Tip
☃ The night before, spray 9 x 13-inch
casserole dish and place hash browns
evenly in dish. Sprinkle with melted
butter, salt, and pepper, and cover with
plastic wrap.

☃ Whisk eggs and milk together and store in
covered bowl.

☃ Use cubed ham and preshredded cheese
that has been frozen. Take out of freezer
and place in refrigerator to defrost
overnight.

Double-Duty Cooking Tip
☃ Cube one extra ham steak and place
cubed ham in the freezer for use in
another recipe.

⸎ **Cinnamon Puffins** ⸎

By Shanna Allen

Prep Time: 15 minutes

Total Cooking Time: 20 minutes

Fast-Food Meal Prep Time: 10 minutes

Serves: 6–12

Approximate Calories per Serving: 325

Ingredients

1½ cups all-purpose flour

1½ tsp. baking powder

½ tsp. salt

½ tsp. ground nutmeg

⅓ cup shortening

½ cup sugar

1 egg

1 tsp. vanilla extract

½ cup milk

Toppings

½ cup butter

½ tsp. ground nutmeg

½ cup sugar

1 tsp. ground cinnamon

Method

Lightly grease a 12-cup muffin pan. Preheat oven to 350°. Into one bowl combine flour, baking powder, salt, and ½ tsp. nutmeg. In another bowl beat shortening, ½ cup sugar, egg, and vanilla until blended. Add the flour mixture to the creamed mixture and beat in the milk until smooth. Fill each cup of the muffin pan ⅔ full with batter. Bake 20 minutes or until light golden brown. In the meantime, melt butter in a small pan or microwave. In a separate small bowl, combine ½ cup sugar, cinnamon, and ½ tsp. nutmeg. While puffins are still warm from taking out of the oven, dip the top of each muffin into the melted butter, then in sugar mixture, coating thoroughly. Cool and store in airtight container. Makes 1 dozen.

Tools Needed

12-cup muffin pan

Two mixing bowls

Large spoon

Measuring cups

Measuring spoons

Side Dishes

Scrambled eggs

Fresh fruit

Fast-Food Kitchen Tip

⇥ Defrost prefrozen muffins. Serve with breakfast.

⇥ Use premeasured dry ingredients.

Double-Duty Cooking Tip

⇥ Double the recipe. Flash-freeze and save extra muffins in FoodSaver bags (4 to a bag) for a breakfast meal later.

❧ Fast and Easy Breakfast Casserole ❧

Prep Time: 15 minutes
Total Cooking Time: 35 minutes
Fast-Food Meal Prep Time: 7 minutes

Serves: 8 generously
Approximate Calories per Serving: 500

Ingredients

6–8 hash brown squares (frozen)

1 lb. bacon, sausage, or ham, cooked and crumbled or cut into small bite-sized pieces, or a combination of meats

6 eggs, beaten

1 cup cheddar cheese, shredded (or any cheese you like)

1 cup onion, chopped (optional)

Method

Preheat oven to 350°. Spray a 9 x 13-inch casserole pan with cooking spray. Line with the frozen hash browns. Spread the cooked meat on top. Pour beaten eggs over the top and sprinkle cheese and onions on the top. Bake for 30–35 minutes.

Optional toppings: Sour cream, avocado slices, chopped green chilies, salsa

Tools Needed

9 x 13-inch casserole dish
Measuring cups
Whisk
Bowl for cracking and whisking eggs

Side Dishes

Fresh fruit
Biscuits

Fast-Food Kitchen Tip

⇾ Use precut, chopped or cubed bacon, sausage, or ham.

⇾ Use preshredded cheese.

⇾ Use prechopped onion.

Double-Duty Cooking Tip

⇾ Cook extra bacon and sausage and freeze in FoodSaver bag for another recipe later in the month.

⇾ Chop 1 extra onion and freeze in FoodSaver bag.

⇾ Shred extra cheese and freeze in a FoodSaver bag.

French Toast Casserole

By Tammy Windham

Prep Time: 15 minutes
Total Cooking Time: 45 minutes
Fast-Food Meal Prep Time: 15 minutes

Serves: 4 generously
Approximate Calories per Serving: 400

Ingredients

10 slices bread—remove the crust.
    Depending on the size of the bread, you
    may need fewer slices for the two layers.
2 pkgs. (8 oz. each) cream cheese, cut into
    small cubes (may use lite cream cheese)
12 eggs
2 cups milk
1 tsp. vanilla
1 tsp. cinnamon
⅓ cup maple syrup
Dash of salt

Method

Spray 9 x 13-inch casserole pan with
cooking spray. Layer half of the bread in
the bottom of the pan. Top with the cream
cheese cubes. Add the remaining bread
on top. Whisk together the eggs and milk.
Mix in salt, vanilla, cinnamon, and maple
syrup. Pour this mixture over the bread and
cheese mixture. Cover with plastic wrap and
refrigerate overnight. Bake at 375° for 45
minutes. Sprinkle with powdered sugar and
serve with syrup.

Tools Needed

9 x 13-inch casserole pan
Whisk
Paring or butter knife (for removing crust)
Measuring cups
Measuring spoons

Side Dishes

Hash browns
Bacon, ham, or sausage

Fast-Food Kitchen Tip

⇥ Assemble the night before, ready to cook
    in the morning. Great for entertaining
    guests.

Double-Duty Cooking Tip

⇥ Save bread crusts and freeze to be used for
    bread crumbs.

Muesli Breakfast Mix

By Tracy Calzaretta

Prep Time: 15 minutes

Total Cooking Time: 0 minutes

Fast-Food Meal Prep Time: 5 minutes

Serves: 8–12 generously

Approximate Calories per Serving: 500

Ingredients

Mix together the following:

3 cups steel-cut oatmeal (available at Trader Joe's)

1 cup skim milk powder

½ cup flax meal (or bran meal)

1 cup coconut

2 cups raisins

2 cups chopped apricots

1–2 cups chopped nuts (pecans, pine nuts, walnuts, and so on)

½ cup brown sugar

1–2 cups sunflower seeds (your choice)

You may add or substitute ingredients of your choice.

Method

To serve: Measure out one cup of the mixture above. For each 1 cup of the muesli mixture, add ½ cup heavy cream, sour cream, or milk. Let sit for 30–40 minutes. Add fresh berries or other fresh fruit. Add a dollop of sour cream or whipped cream and drizzle with honey. You can add more milk or water if you like it less dense. If you don't have time to wait, you can add the cream or milk and fruit and eat immediately. Also a great addition to nonfat yogurt.

It's even better after a day or two!

Tools Needed

Large storage bowl with airtight lid (preferably Tupperware or Rubbermaid with airtight lids)

Large mixing bowl

Large spoon

Measuring cups

Side Dishes

Juice

Fast-Food Kitchen Tip

⇥ Use premeasured mixture. Scoop out mixture into bowls with lids before bed. Add the cream or milk and place in the refrigerator, ready to eat in the morning. Add fresh berries for a well-balanced meal.

Double-Duty Cooking Tip

⇥ Make a double mixture to have on hand for a quick meal for breakfast. Also a great idea for a lunch meal.

❧ Nutty Banana Chocolate Pancakes ❧

Prep Time: 15 minutes

Total Cooking Time: 15 minutes

Fast-Food Meal Prep Time: 10 minutes

Serves: 4 generously

Approximate Calories per Serving: 400

Ingredients
1 cup all-purpose flour
2 tsp. baking powder
¼ tsp. salt
1 tsp. baking soda
¾ cup milk
3 T. butter, melted
2 large eggs
1 T. sugar
1 tsp. vanilla extract
1 large ripe banana, cut into small pieces
½ cup miniature chocolate chips
¼ cup chopped walnuts (or pecans)

Method
Combine dry ingredients, set aside. Whisk together the milk, melted butter, sugar, eggs, and vanilla. Add to dry ingredients and mix, but do not overmix. Fold in the banana, chocolate chips, and nuts.

Heat griddle on medium heat, spray with cooking spray, and pour batter on hot griddle. Cook until bubbles appear and then flip. Serve with whipped cream and syrup.

Tools Needed
Griddle
Mixing bowl
Whisk
Large spoon
Measuring cups
Measuring spoons
Butter knife

Side Dishes
Bacon, ham, or sausage
Fresh fruit

Fast-Food Kitchen Tip
- Reheat frozen pancakes for a quick breakfast on a busy morning.

- Use pancake mix instead of scratch pancakes and add only the vanilla, banana, chocolate chips, and nuts (optional).

Double-Duty Cooking Tip
- Cook 4–5 extra pancakes and cool to room temperature. Flash-freeze and store in FoodSaver bag. Separate with wax paper.

- Make up extra pancake batter and store in an airtight container in the refrigerator. Can be stored in the refrigerator for up to one week. Ready to add different add-ins such as fruit or chocolate chips.

⚜ Overnight French Toast ⚜

Submitted by Robin Fitzsimons

Prep Time: 15 minutes

Total Cooking Time: 40 minutes

Fast-Food Meal Prep Time: 15 minutes

Serves: 6–8 generously

Approximate Calories per Serving: 450

Ingredients

1 stick butter (½ cup)

1 cup brown sugar

1 tsp. cinnamon

6 eggs

1½ cups milk

1 loaf bread (you won't use the whole loaf)

Method

Melt butter into 9 x 13-inch pan. Mix brown sugar and cinnamon together. Sprinkle evenly on top of melted butter. Place slices of bread 2 inches thick on top of butter and brown sugar mixture. Beat eggs and milk together. Pour over bread. Cover with plastic wrap (not foil) and refrigerate overnight. Next morning, uncover and bake at 300° for 30–40 minutes. Serve with warmed syrup.

You can use any type of bread, but cinnamon raisin bread is delicious!

Tools Needed

9 x 13-inch casserole pan

Measuring cups

Measuring spoons

Large mixing bowl

Whisk

Side Dishes

Fresh fruit

Bacon, sausage, or ham

Fast-Food Kitchen Tip

⇥ Assemble the night before. Cut up fresh fruit and cook bacon or sausage if serving.

Double-Duty Cooking Tip

⇥ Make an extra casserole to serve later in the week. Use casserole dish with a cover. Cover the casserole dish with plastic wrap lid. Keep no longer than 3–4 days in the refrigerator before cooking.

Peanut Butter, Banana, and Honey Muffins

Prep Time: 15 minutes

Total Cooking Time: 0 minutes

Fast-Food Meal Prep Time: 15 minutes

Serves: 4

Approximate Calories per Serving: 300

Ingredients
4 English muffins, toasted
4 T. peanut butter
1 banana, sliced
4 tsp. honey

Method
Lightly toast English muffins. Spread one half with 1 tsp. honey, 1 T. peanut butter, and cover with banana slices. Place other half of muffin on top for a delicious and nutritious breakfast sandwich.

Tools Needed
Measuring spoons
Butter knife
Paring knife

Side Dishes
Juice or milk

Fast-Food Kitchen Tip
➢ Prepare the sandwiches with everything but the bananas before bed. Wrap tightly in plastic wrap and place in the refrigerator. In the morning, place in the microwave oven for 10–15 seconds. Open and place sliced bananas inside. Ready to eat in a minute!

Double-Duty Cooking Tip
➢ Make up 4 extra sandwiches without the bananas. Wrap tightly in plastic wrap. Flash-freeze for an hour and place in a FoodSaver bag. Thaw and place in the microwave for 10–15 seconds. Open and add the bananas. Great for road trips.

Peanut Butter and Banana Breakfast Cups

Prep Time: 15 minutes

Total Cooking Time: 0 minutes

Fast-Food Meal Prep Time: 5–7 minutes

Serves: 4

Approximate Calories per Serving: 285

Ingredients

1¾ cups plain, low-fat yogurt

2 T. smooth peanut butter

1–2 T. honey (or sweet agave)

1 large banana, sliced

2 cups lightly sweetened multigrain clusters
(cereal) or granola

Method

Whisk together the yogurt, peanut butter, and honey until creamy and smooth. Evenly divide this mixture into four glasses or custard cups. (If possible, use chilled glasses.) Top all four glasses evenly with half the sliced bananas, and half the clusters or granola. Repeat this one more time. Serve immediately.

Tools Needed

Four glasses or custard cups

Whisk

Mixing bowl

Measuring cups

Measuring spoons

Side Dishes

Buttered toast

Fast-Food Kitchen Tip

⇨ Prepare yogurt mixture the night before and refrigerate overnight. Assemble when ready to eat. Saves time in the morning!

Double-Duty Cooking Tip

⇨ Make up 1 extra recipe of yogurt mixture and store in the refrigerator in a large covered container. Use within 1 week.

⇨ Measure out 2 extra servings of multigrain clusters or granola. Store in a FoodSaver bag and freeze. Can use immediately the next time you make this recipe.

❧ South of the Border Egg Casserole ❧

Prep Time: 15 minutes

Total Cooking Time: 25–30 minutes

Fast-Food Meal Prep Time: 10 minutes

Serves: 6 generously

Approximate Calories per Serving: 425

Ingredients

2 cups cornbread stuffing mix

1 can (15 oz.) whole kernel corn, drained well (can use Mexican corn if desired)

1 can chopped green chilies—do not drain

½ cup sour cream

7 eggs

1 cup shredded cheese (Monterey Jack or cheddar)

Optional toppings: Sour cream, avocados, chopped onion, sliced black olives, salsa

Tools Needed

9 x 13-inch casserole dish

Mixing bowl

Measuring cups

Can opener

Large spoon

Method

Preheat oven to 400°. Spray a 9 x 13-inch dish with cooking spray.

Mix together the stuffing, canned corn, green chilies, sour cream, and 1 egg. Spread evenly in the prepared 9 x 13-inch pan.

Take a large wooden spoon and make six indentations evenly in the pan—two rows of three. Break one egg into each pouch. With a fork, pierce the yolk of each egg. Bake uncovered for 20–25 minutes until the egg yolks and egg whites are cooked and firm, not runny. Sprinkle cheese over the top and bake for 3 minutes longer, and the cheese is melted.

Side Dishes

Fresh fruit

Bacon, ham, or sausage

Fast-Food Kitchen Tip

⇥ Use preshredded cheese.

Double-Duty Cooking Tip

⇥ Grate an extra cup of cheddar cheese and freeze for use later in another recipe.

Comment

⇥ Can be served for breakfast, lunch, or dinner.

Spicy Scrambled Eggs

Prep Time: 15–25 minutes

Total Cooking Time: 7 minutes

Fast-Food Meal Prep Time: 10 minutes

Serves: 4 generously

Approximate Calories per Serving: 375

Ingredients

½ cup chopped onion
¼ cup chopped red bell pepper
1 jalapeño pepper, seeded and finely chopped
8 pieces of bacon, cooked crisp and crumbled
8 eggs, beaten
1 cup shredded cheddar cheese
½ tsp. salt
⅛ tsp. pepper

Method

In a large skillet, spray nonstick cooking spray and sauté the onion and peppers until tender, approximately 3 minutes. Add the cooked and crumbled bacon to the skillet. Pour the beaten eggs over the top of the bacon and veggies. Sprinkle ½ cup of the shredded cheddar cheese and the salt and pepper. Cook on low to medium heat until the egg mixture is set. Stir often. Sprinkle with the remaining ½ cup of cheddar cheese and serve immediately.

Tools Needed

Large skillet
Paring knife
Spatula
Measuring cups
Measuring spoons

Side Dishes

Salsa
Sour cream
Sliced avocado
Muffins or biscuits
Fresh fruit

Fast-Food Kitchen Tip

⤷ Use prechopped onion and pepper.

⤷ Use prechopped jalapeño.

⤷ Use preshredded cheese.

⤷ Use precooked and crumbled bacon.

Double-Duty Cooking Tip

⤷ Chop extra onion and bell pepper and freeze in a FoodSaver bag for use later in the month.

⤷ Chop an extra jalapeño and freeze in a FoodSaver bag for use later in the month.

⤷ Shred extra cheese and freeze in a FoodSaver bag.

⤷ Cook extra bacon and crumble. Store and freeze in a FoodSaver bag.

Spicy Scrambled Eggs and Veggie Sandwiches

Prep Time: 15 minutes

Total Cooking Time: 10 minutes

Fast-Food Meal Prep Time: 5 minutes

Serves: 4

Approximate Calories per Serving: 425

Ingredients

⅓ cup chopped green pepper

¼ cup chopped onion

6 eggs (may use half eggs and half egg whites)

1 T. milk or water

¼ tsp. ground mustard

Salt and pepper to taste

⅛ tsp. hot pepper sauce

⅓ cup fresh or frozen corn (thawed)

¼ cup real bacon bits (can use real bacon if preferred)

Sliced cheddar cheese (optional)

4 English muffins, split and toasted

Method

Spray skillet with nonstick spray and cook pepper and onion until tender. In a large bowl, whisk eggs together with milk, salt and pepper, mustard, pepper sauce; pour into skillet. Add corn and bacon and cook until eggs are completely set. Spoon onto toasted English muffin bottoms; replace tops. Serve immediately.

Tools Needed

Skillet

Bowl

Whisk

Large spoon

Measuring cups

Measuring spoons

Side Dishes

Hash browns

Fresh fruit

Fast-Food Kitchen Tip

⤏ Use precut onion and bell pepper.

⤏ Use precooked bacon.

Double-Duty Cooking Tip

⤏ Chop extra portion of onion and bell pepper and save for another use.

Main Dishes

❧ 1-2-3 Meat Loaf ❧

Prep Time: 10 minutes
Total Cooking Time: 45–50 minutes or
    17 minutes in the microwave

Fast-Food Meal Prep Time: 10 minutes
Serves: 6–8
Approximate Calories per Serving: 400

Ingredients
1½ lbs. lean ground beef or turkey
1 pkg. (6 oz.) Stove Top Chicken Stuffing
2 large eggs
1 cup + 2 T. ketchup

Method
Mix together all ingredients and pat into
an 8 x 8-inch glass baking dish. Brush
2 T. ketchup over the top. Bake at 350° for
45–50 minutes. *Microwave Instructions:* This
meat loaf recipe can also be cooked in the
microwave. Place in 8 x 8-inch glass baking
dish and microwave on high for 7 minutes.
Turn a quarter turn and cook on high an
additional 8–10 minutes. (If you use a
different size pan such as a loaf pan, cooking
times will need to be increased.) This is a real
favorite with kids.

Optional add-ins: Chopped onions, chopped
green chilies

Tools Needed
8 x 8-inch glass baking dish
Measuring cup
Measuring spoon

Side Dishes
Mashed potatoes or rice
Green beans
Rolls

Fast-Food Kitchen Tip
❧ Use prefrozen, uncooked meat loaf.
Defrost in the microwave or on the
counter and cook as directed above.

Double-Duty Cooking Tip
❧ Prepare a double batch and freeze half
(uncooked) in a FoodSaver bag.

❧ When ready to serve for another meal,
defrost and press into an 8 x 8-inch glass
casserole dish. Cook as directed above.

❧ Baked Chicken Strips ❧

Prep Time: 15 minutes
Total Cooking Time: 15 minutes
Fast-Food Meal Prep Time: 5 minutes

Serves: 4 generously
Approximate Calories per Serving
  (2 strips): 350

Ingredients

1 lb. boneless, skinless chicken breasts, cut
  into strips
¼–½ cup buttermilk (mayonnaise can be
  used instead of buttermilk)
1 cup seasoned bread crumbs
½ tsp. garlic powder
½ tsp. paprika
2 tsp. Italian seasoning
½ tsp. salt

Method

Combine dry ingredients. Pat dry the
chicken strips with paper towels. Dip into
buttermilk and then dredge through bread
crumb mixture. Place on a baking sheet or
stone. Bake for 15 minutes in an oven set
at 425°. Thoroughly clean area where raw
chicken has touched with warm sudsy water.
Wash hands thoroughly with soap and water.

Tools Needed

Measuring cups
Measuring spoons
Baking stone or cookie sheet
Kitchen scissors

Side Dishes

Rice or potato dish
Green salad
Rolls

Fast-Food Kitchen Tip

❧ Use premeasured dry ingredients.

❧ Use precut chicken strips.

Double-Duty Cooking Tip

❧ Measure extra dry ingredients into small
  containers and refrigerate or freeze them
  for future use.

❧ Cut up extra chicken and freeze for
  another meal later in the week or month.

Baked Parmesan Chicken

Prep Time: 15 minutes

Total Cooking Time: 45 minutes–1 hour

Fast-Food Meal Prep Time: 10 minutes

Serves: 6

Approximate Calories per Serving: 450

Ingredients

1 stick butter (½ cup), melted

1 cup soft, Italian seasoned bread crumbs

½ cup grated Parmesan cheese

6 boneless, skinless chicken breasts (if frozen, thaw and pat dry)

Method

Melt butter in the microwave in a microwave-safe bowl, approximately 1 minute. Mix together the bread crumbs and Parmesan cheese in a mixing bowl. Dip both sides of the chicken in the butter and then dredge both sides of the chicken in the crumb mixture. Spray a light coat of cooking spray in the bottom of a 9 x 13 inch casserole dish. Lay the chicken breasts in the pan and bake at 350° for 45 minutes–1 hour. Turn chicken breasts one time halfway through cooking time. If chicken begins to brown too quickly, cover with foil after about 40 minutes.

Tools Needed

9 x 13-inch casserole dish

2 mixing bowls

Measuring cups

Side Dishes

White or brown rice

Steamed broccoli, asparagus, or green beans

Sliced tomatoes

Fast-Food Kitchen Tip

- Line the bottom of the 9 x 13-inch casserole dish with aluminum foil for easy cleanup.

- Use premixed bowl of bread crumbs and cheese from the freezer.

Double-Duty Cooking Tip

- Mix up extra bread crumbs and Parmesan cheese and store in a FoodSaver bag and freeze for use in this recipe later in the next 1–2 months.

❧ Baked Sloppy Joes ❧

Prep Time: 30 minutes

Total Cooking Time: 20 minutes

Fast-Food Meal Prep Time: 10 minutes

Serves: 4 generously

Approximate Calories per Serving: 400

Ingredients

1 lb. ground beef (or turkey)
1 chopped onion (optional)
1 can (15.5 oz.) sloppy joe sauce
1 (11 oz.) can Mexicorn (reserve ⅓ cup)
1 cup all-purpose baking mix (Bisquick)
¾ cup shredded cheddar cheese
⅓ cup water

Method

Preheat oven to 425°. Coat a 1½-quart baking dish with cooking spray. In large nonstick skillet, cook meat and onion over medium heat until meat is browned and onion is tender, about 5 minutes. Drain excess fat, stir in sloppy joe sauce, and cook until heated through; remove from heat. Reserve ⅓ cup Mexicorn, stir remaining into meat mixture and transfer to baking dish. Stir baking mix, ½ cup cheese, and ⅓ cup water into reserved Mexicorn. Dollop spoonfuls over meat mixture. Bake 15–20 minutes or until biscuits are golden, sprinkling with remaining cheese during last 2 minutes of cooking. Cool 10 minutes.

Optional toppings: Sour cream and avocado slices. Enjoy!

Tools Needed

Baking dish
Can opener
Measuring cups

Side Dishes

Fresh fruit
Green beans or cauliflower

Fast-Food Kitchen Tip

⊁ Use precooked ground beef; defrost.

⊁ Use prechopped onion.

Double-Duty Cooking Tip

⊁ Cook extra ground beef or turkey and freeze in 1-lb. packages. (2 cups cooked ground beef or turkey equals 1 lb.)

⊁ Chop 2 onions and freeze onion in a FoodSaver bag for use later in the week or month.

Barbecue Camp Burgers

Prep Time: 15 minutes

Total Cooking Time: 7–10 minutes

Fast-Food Meal Prep Time: 10 minutes

Serves: 6–8

Approximate Calories per Serving: 500

Ingredients
2 lbs. lean ground beef

Salt and pepper

2 cups each of various vegetables, chopped into chunks—onion, celery, carrots, bell pepper, broccoli, cauliflower, zucchini, potatoes, and any other vegetable favorites

Method
Make hamburger patties (¼–⅓ lb. each) and salt and pepper to taste. Tear two sheets of heavy duty aluminum foil (approximately 12 x 12 inches) for each burger. Lay the seasoned meat patty on one sheet of aluminum foil. Each person adds their favorite vegetables and seasons with additional salt and pepper. Place the second sheet of aluminum foil on top and tightly seal completely around. Place the aluminum foil package on barbecue grill and cook for approximately 7–10 minutes. DO NOT OPEN. For larger patties, cook a little longer. The moisture and heat inside the foil cooks the ground beef patty and steams the vegetables. Use tongs to remove packages and transfer to a plate. Open carefully so as not to be burned by the steam. Great for backyard barbecues or camping.

Tools Needed
Measuring cup

Several small bowls for vegetables

Paring knife

Aluminum foil

Side Dishes
Fresh fruit

Pasta salad

Fast-Food Kitchen Tip
- Use premade patties that have been frozen. Thaw before cooking.

- Use prechopped vegetables.

Double-Duty Cooking Tip
- Make up several extra patties and freeze in a FoodSaver bag.

- If using this recipe a second time later in the week, chop extra vegetables and store in a FoodSaver bag in the refrigerator for up to 1 week.

❧ Cheddar Potato Chowder ❧

Prep Time: 15 minutes

Total Cooking Time: 30 minutes

Fast-Food Meal Prep Time: 7–10 minutes

Serves: 4

Approximate Calories per Serving: 600

Ingredients

3 T. butter

3 medium carrots, sliced

2 medium celery stalks, sliced thin

1 small onion, finely chopped

3 T. flour

¼ tsp. dry mustard

¼ tsp. paprika

¼ tsp. pepper

2 cups milk

2 cups water

4 medium potatoes, peeled and cut into
   ½-inch cubes

2 chicken flavored bouillon cubes

1½ cups shredded cheddar cheese

Method

In a 3-quart saucepan over medium heat, melt butter. Add carrots, celery, and onion. Cook until tender, approximately 10 minutes, stirring occasionally. Stir in the flour, mustard, paprika, and pepper. Cook for one minute. Gradually add milk, water, potatoes, and bouillon. Bring to a boil over high heat. Reduce heat to low. Cover and simmer for 10 minutes or until the potatoes are tender. Remove from heat. Add the cheese and stir just until the cheese has melted.

Optional toppings: Crumbled bacon and finely chopped chives

Tools Needed

Large saucepan

Measuring cups

Measuring spoons

Large spoon

Paring knife

Side Dishes

Dinner rolls or breadsticks

Green salad

Fast-Food Kitchen Tip

⤙ Use precut and sliced vegetables.

⤙ Use preshredded cheese.

⤙ Use unpeeled potatoes.

Double-Duty Cooking Tip

⤙ Cut extra vegetables and store in a FoodSaver bag in the refrigerator for up to 2 weeks for use in another recipe.

⤙ Shred extra cheese and freeze in a FoodSaver bag.

⤙ Double the recipe and store extra soup in large mugs with lids for a quick meal on a busy night later in the week or month. Leave room at the top of the mug for expansion in the freezer.

⚜ Chicken and Rice Casserole ⚜

Prep Time: 15 minutes

Total Cooking Time: 1½ hours

Fast-Food Meal Prep Time: 10 minutes

Serves: 4–6 generously

Approximate Calories per Serving: 425

Ingredients

1 envelope dry onion soup mix
1 can (10¾ oz.) cream of mushroom soup
2¼ cups water
1 cup long grain rice, uncooked (not instant)
1 whole chicken, cut up or 4 boneless,
    skinless chicken breasts

Method

If using the oven, preheat to 350°. Blend dry soup mix with mushroom soup and water. Pour rice in a lightly greased 9 x 13-inch baking pan and pour half of the soup mixture over the rice. Place chicken on rice, skin side up (if using a whole chicken). Season with salt and pepper to taste and then cover with remaining soup mixture. Bake 1–1½ hours till done. *If using Crock-Pot,* lightly grease bottom, place rice in bottom of the Crock-Pot, layer the chicken over the rice, and then pour soup mixture on the top. Cook on high for 3–4 hours or low for 6–8 hours.

Tools Needed

9 x 13-inch pan or Crock-Pot
Measuring cups
Large spoon
Bowl for mixing sauce ingredients
Can opener

Side Dishes

Green salad
Biscuits or rolls

Fast-Food Kitchen Tip

⚜ Reheat frozen Chicken and Rice Casserole in microwave oven in a microwave safe dish.

Double-Duty Cooking Tip

⚜ Double the recipe and save half for a meal later in the month. Freeze in a large freezer bag.

Comments

⚜ This is an excellent recipe for the oven or the Crock-Pot. You can use frozen boneless, skinless chicken breasts when using the Crock-Pot. This will reduce the fat and calories.

⚜ Keep a supply of the other ingredients on hand for a quick meal idea.

❧ Chicken Chowder ❧

Submitted by Peggy Means

Prep Time: 15 minutes

Total Cooking Time: 1–1½ hours

Fast-Food Meal Prep Time: 10 minutes

Serves: 6–8 generously

Approximate Calories per Serving: 400

Ingredients

2 cans (14 oz. each) chicken broth

4–5 medium potatoes, diced

1 can (14.5 oz.) creamed corn

1 can (14.5 oz.) whole kernel corn, drained

1 can (15 oz.) diced tomatoes

1 can (8 oz.) tomato sauce

1–2 cups cooked chicken

Salt, pepper, onion powder to taste

Method

Cook potatoes in chicken broth in large
Dutch oven or large stockpot until tender.
Combine remaining ingredients and simmer
for 30 minutes.

Tools Needed

Dutch oven or large stockpot

Can opener

Measuring cup

Paring knife

Side Dishes

Crackers, rolls or cornbread

Fresh fruit

Fast-Food Kitchen Tip

⊰⊱ Don't peel the potatoes, simply dice with
the skin on for a more nutritious meal.

⊰⊱ Use canned chicken.

⊰⊱ Use rotisserie chicken.

Double-Duty Cooking Tip

⊰⊱ Save extra soup in individual food-safe
bowls and freeze for a quick meal on a
busy night. Leave ½ inch at the top of the
bowl to allow for expansion in the freezer.
Defrost and heat in the microwave.

⊰⊱ If using a rotisserie chicken, save an extra
recipe serving in a FoodSaver bag and
freeze for use in another recipe.

⚜ Chicken Enchilada Casserole ⚜

Prep Time: 15 minutes

Total Cooking Time: 40 minutes (oven)
or 2–3 hours (Crock-Pot)

Fast-Food Meal Prep Time: 10 minutes

Serves: 8 generously

Approximate Calories per Serving: 525

Ingredients

3 chicken breasts, cubed, or 3 large cans
chicken breast meat, or rotisserie chicken
2 cans (15 oz. each) enchilada sauce
12–15 corn tortillas
3 cups shredded cheese
Chopped onions (optional)
Chopped or sliced olives (optional)

Method

Preheat oven to 350°. Grease bottom of
9 x 13-inch casserole dish. Pour enchilada
sauce to cover bottom. Layer with tortillas,
then add chicken, more sauce, cheese, olives,
and onions (if desired). Continue with 2 to 3
more layers. Top off with extra cheese. Bake
casserole for approximately 30–40 minutes or
until hot completely through. Garnish with
sour cream and/or avocado slices.

May be heated in the microwave if prepared
in a glass casserole or microwave-safe dish.
Freezes well.

Can be layered in a Crock-Pot and cooked
on low for 2–3 hours (if using previously
cooked chicken). Garnish with extra cheese
before serving.

Tools Needed

9 x 13-inch casserole dish
Measuring cup
Can opener
Paring knife

Side Dishes

Spanish rice
Refried beans

Fast-Food Kitchen Tip

⚜ Use prechopped onion.

⚜ Use preshredded cheese.

⚜ Use precubed chicken or canned chicken
breast, drained well.

Double-Duty Cooking Tip

⚜ Double the recipe and freeze half for a
meal later in the week or month. Can also
be frozen in individual serving sizes by
placing a 3-inch square on a plate (freezer-
and microwave-safe). Add a scoop of
Spanish rice and freeze for a homemade
dinner for an evening when Mom will be
gone or out on a date night with Dad. I
like to use square salad-sized plates. They
fit perfectly in a large FoodSaver bag and
can be frozen individually.

❧ Chicken Pesto Pasta ❧

Prep Time: 15 minutes

Total Cooking Time: 30 minutes

Fast-Food Meal Prep Time: 10 minutes

Serves: 6–8

Approximate Calories per Serving: 575

Ingredients

4 boneless, skinless chicken breasts, cooked and cubed

2 T. olive oil

1 container favorite pesto sauce

1 box bow tie pasta

Parmesan cheese (optional)

Method

Heat olive oil in a large skillet. Add chicken breasts, turning every 5 minutes. Cook until done. Once cooked, take out, drain on paper towels, and set aside to cool. While chicken is cooking, prepare pasta per package directions in a large saucepan. Drain, rinse with hot water, and return to saucepan. Add pesto sauce and mix well. When chicken has cooled, use kitchen scissors and cut into cubes. Add to the pesto and pasta. Warm if necessary. Sprinkle Parmesan cheese on warm pasta.

Tools Needed

Large skillet

Large saucepan

Measuring spoon

Kitchen scissors

Strainer

Side Dishes

Garlic bread or toast

Green salad

Fast-Food Kitchen Tip

✂ Use precooked pasta.

✂ Use precooked and cubed chicken breast.

Double-Duty Cooking Tip

✂ Cook 3 or 4 extra chicken breasts, cool, and cube. Put into a FoodSaver bag and freeze for use later in the week or month.

✂ Cook 1 extra box of pasta. Drain and rinse. Cool to room temperature and store in a FoodSaver bag. Can be refrigerated for up to 4 weeks in the refrigerator (do not freeze).

Chicken Taco Pizza

Prep Time: 15 minutes
Total Cooking Time: 15–25 minutes
Fast-Food Meal Prep Time: 10 minutes

Serves: 4–6 generously (1 pizza)
Approximate Calories per Serving: 425

Ingredients

1 frozen cheese pizza (choose your family's favorite)
¾ cup taco sauce
1½ cups cooked chicken, chopped (may use canned chicken, drain well)
¾ cup canned or frozen corn (frozen roasted corn is great for this recipe)
1 cup Mexican-style shredded cheese
Cilantro, chopped (optional)

Method

Preheat oven to 400°. Line a pizza pan with foil or parchment paper and spray with Pam. Place pizza on pan and spread taco sauce evenly. Combine chicken, corn, and cilantro (optional) and spoon over pizza. Bake for 15 minutes or until thoroughly heated. Sprinkle with cheese, bake an additional 5 minutes.

Optional garnishes: Sliced olives, sliced avocado, sliced jalapeños, sour cream

Tools Needed

Large flat pizza pan or round baking stone
Measuring cups
Pizza cutter

Side Dishes

Fresh fruit
Green salad

Fast-Food Kitchen Tip

- Use precooked and chopped chicken.
- Use preshredded cheese or packaged, shredded cheese.
- Use frozen, roasted corn.

Double-Duty Cooking Tip

- Cilantro can be chopped and placed in a small bowl with a tight-fitting lid and stored in the freezer. Use on any recipe that calls for cilantro.
- Cook 2–3 chicken breasts and cut into small, bite-sized pieces. Freeze ½ to ¾ cup serving sizes in FoodSaver bags to have on hand for pizzas later in the week or month.
- Keep 2–3 extra-large cheese pizzas or small individual pizzas on hand, along with the other ingredients, for a quick fast-food meal for a busy evening.

Chicken Tenders with
Trader Joe's Double Roasted Salsa

Prep Time: 5 minutes

Total Cooking Time: 6–8 hours

Fast-Food Meal Prep Time: 5 minutes

Serves: 4–6 generously

Approximate Calories per Serving: 250

Ingredients

8–10 frozen chicken breast tenders (boneless, skinless)

1 jar Trader Joe's Double Roasted Salsa

Method

Place chicken tenders into the Crock-Pot and pour the salsa on top. Cover and cook on low for 6–8 hours.

Tools Needed

Crock-Pot

Side Dishes

Rice

Green salad

Fast-Food Kitchen Tip

⊰ Use presaved salsa chicken. Reheat in microwave or in the Crock-Pot.

Double-Duty Cooking Tip

⊰ Cook extra in the Crock-Pot and freeze extra portion in a large freezer container for another meal later in the week. Serve inside tortillas with shredded lettuce, cheese, and avocado.

❧ Chili Spaghetti ❧

Prep Time: 15 minutes

Total Cooking Time: 10–12 minutes

Fast-Food Meal Cooking Time: 5 minutes

Serves: 4 generously

Approximate Calories per Serving: 475

Ingredients
8 ounces pasta (bow tie pasta works well)
1 can chili without beans
½ onion, chopped
1 cup cheddar cheese, shredded
Salsa (optional)

Method
Cook spaghetti noodles according to package directions; drain well. Heat chili in a saucepan or warm in the microwave. Pour warmed chili over noodles and mix well. Top noodles and chili with onions, cheese, and salsa (optional) according to taste. Add sliced avocados to the top if desired. Can be served over steamed tamales. Add 1 cup cubed chicken or ½ lb. ground beef for a heartier meal.

Tools Needed
Large pot (for preparing pasta and then used to mix ingredients)
Can opener
Measuring cup
Knife

Side Dishes
Tortilla chips
Tamales
Fresh watermelon (or other fruit)

Fast-Food Kitchen Tip
- Use precooked pasta. Refresh with boiling water in strainer.

- Use prechopped onion. Remove from refrigerator or freezer in the morning.

- Use preshredded cheese. Remove from refrigerator or freezer in the morning.

Double-Duty Cooking Tip
- Cook an extra serving of pasta and place in FoodSaver bag and refrigerate (do not freeze). To refresh for another recipe, simply pour boiling water over pasta in a strainer.

- Chop 1 extra onion and store in FoodSaver bag for use later on in the week or month. Refrigerate or freeze.

- Shred extra cheese and save for use later. Refrigerate or freeze.

- Prepare a double portion and save half for a meal later in the week or month.

❧ Creamy Chicken Quiche ❧

Prep Time: 20 minutes

Total Cooking Time: 1 hour

Fast-Food Meal Prep Time: 10 minutes

Serves: 4–6 generously

Approximate Calories per Serving: 600

Ingredients

1 frozen pie crust, thawed (9-inch)
1 T. olive oil
¼ cup onion, chopped
¼ cup green bell pepper, chopped
1 T. all-purpose flour
1 cup cubed chicken breast
¼ tsp. salt
¼ tsp. nutmeg
¼ tsp. pepper
½ cup shredded cheddar cheese
¼ cup shredded Swiss cheese
2 eggs
¾ cup milk
¾ cup sour cream

Method

Place thawed pie crust in a 9-inch pie plate. Refrigerate until ready to use.

In a medium skillet, heat olive oil. Add onion and bell pepper. Cook 2–3 minutes, stirring often. Add the flour and cook for an additional 2 minutes, stirring often. Next, stir in the chicken, salt, nutmeg, and pepper. Take the pie crust out of the refrigerator and spread this mixture over the bottom of the unbaked crust. Top with the cheeses. In a small bowl, combine eggs, milk, and sour cream. Beat until smooth. Pour over the chicken mixture and place in preheated 400° oven. Bake for 20 minutes; reduce oven temperature to 350° and bake an additional 30–35 minutes. Quiche is ready when a knife inserted in the middle comes out clean.

Tools Needed

Pie pan
Medium skillet
Paring knife
Small bowl
Large spoon
Measuring cups and spoons

Side Dishes

Fresh fruit

Fast-Food Kitchen Tip

⇥ Use precooked and cubed chicken breast or canned chicken breast, drained well.

Double-Duty Cooking Tip

⇥ Cook extra chicken breast and freeze in a FoodSaver bag for use in a recipe later.

⇥ Chop extra bell pepper and onion and freeze in a FoodSaver bag.

⚜ Crock-Pot Artichoke Chicken ⚜

Prep Time: 15 minutes

Total Cooking Time: 6–8 hours

Fast-Food Meal Prep Time: 10 minutes

Serves: 4 generously

Approximate Calories per Serving: 450

Ingredients

1 can (15 oz.) marinated artichoke hearts, drained and chopped fine

¾ cup grated Parmesan cheese (or to taste)

½ cup mayonnaise

½ cup sour cream

4 boneless, skinless chicken breasts

Method

Drain and chop artichokes until fine. Add cheese, mayonnaise, and sour cream. Mix well. Place chicken breasts in the bottom of Crock-Pot and pour artichoke mixture over the top. Cook on low for 6–8 hours. Have extra cheese to put on after serving (optional). Chicken is so tender and delicious. *Note:* You can make this lower in fat and calories by using low- or no-fat mayonnaise and low- or no-fat sour cream.

Tools Needed

Crock-Pot

Can opener

Knife

Measuring cups

Side Dishes

Rice or pasta

Green salad

Green beans

Fast-Food Kitchen Tip

- Use Crock-Pot liner to eliminate messy cleanup.

- Assemble before bedtime and have Crock-Pot ready to plug in and go.

- Use paper bowls. Serve over a scoop of rice.

Double-Duty Cooking Tip

- Cook a double portion and freeze half.

- Mix sauce ahead of time and refrigerate.

- Chop 1–2 extra cans of artichoke hearts and put into FoodSaver bag or other container and refrigerate or freeze.

❧ Crock-Pot Asian Chicken ❧

Prep Time: 15 minutes
Total Cooking Time: 7–8 hours
Fast-Food Meal Prep Time: 10 minutes

Serves: 4–6 generously
Approximate Calories per Serving: 375

Ingredients

12 frozen chicken breast tenders (or 6 chicken breasts)
2 cans (16 oz. each) pineapple chunks (reserve the liquid from 1 can and drain the other)
1 cup teriyaki sauce
1 tsp. minced garlic

Method

Place the chicken tenders (or breasts) in the Crock-Pot. Combine pineapple chunks, juice from 1 can, teriyaki sauce, and garlic. Mix well. Pour over chicken and cook on low for 7–8 hours (on high for 3–4 hours).

Tools Needed

Crock-Pot
Measuring cup
Measuring spoon
Can opener

Side Dishes

White rice
Steamed broccoli or Asian vegetables
Fresh melon slices

Fast-Food Kitchen Tip

➵ Use a Crock-Pot liner for no-hassle cleanup.

➵ Assemble ingredients in the Crock-Pot the night before. Set in the refrigerator. The next morning, all you have to do is put the crock on the heating element and plug it in!

Double-Duty Cooking Tip

➵ Double the recipe and save half for another meal later in the month. Save in a FoodSaver bag and freeze.

➵ Use preminced garlic.

Easy Orange Chicken Fling

By Wilma Glidewell

Prep Time: 10 minutes
Total Cooking Time: 40 minutes
Fast-Food Meal Prep Time: 10 minutes

Serves: 4 generously
Approximate Calories per Serving: 465

Ingredients

4 boneless, skinless chicken breasts (you can
     substitute 6 thighs if you prefer)
1 pkg. Lipton Onion Soup Mix
1 jar orange marmalade

Method

In an 8 x 8-inch casserole dish, *fling* the
chicken in. Then *fling* onion soup mix all
over the top of the chicken. Lastly, *fling* the
orange marmalade by spoonfuls over the
chicken and soup mix. When cooking, the
marmalade will spread over the soup mix
and chicken for a delicious orange-flavored
chicken. Bake at 350° for 30–40 minutes or
until the chicken is done.

Tools Needed

8 x 8-inch casserole dish
Spoon

Side Dishes

Rice
Green beans

Fast-Food Kitchen Tip

- Arrange ingredients in a Crock-Pot and
  cook on low for 6–8 hours. Do not stir.

- Use prefrozen Orange Chicken recipe.
  Thaw and reheat.

Double-Duty Cooking Tip

- Double the recipe and freeze half in a
  FoodSaver bag for a meal later in the
  month.

Fiesta Chicken and Beans

Prep Time: 15 minutes
Total Cooking Time: 20 minutes or 4–6
  hours in Crock-Pot

Fast-Food Meal Prep Time: 5 minutes
Serves: 6
Approximate Calories per Serving: 275

Ingredients

1 lb. uncooked chicken breast, cut into
  chunks
1 pkg. (1 oz.) taco seasoning mix
1 can (11 oz.) Mexicorn (corn with red and
  green peppers)
1 can (15 oz.) black or pinto beans, drained
  and rinsed
½ cup onion, chopped (optional)
¼ cup water

Method

Spray your skillet with nonstick cooking
spray or 1 T. olive oil. Add chicken to the
skillet and cook until no longer pink in the
center (approximately 10 minutes). Stir in
seasoning mix, beans, corn, and water. Cook
over medium-high heat for 10 minutes,
stirring frequently, until sauce thickens. This
recipe may be prepared in a Crock-Pot. Mix
ingredients together in the Crock-Pot and
cook on low for 4–6 hours.

Tools Needed

Skillet or Crock-Pot
Can opener
Measuring cups
Large spoon for stirring
Knife and cutting board for cubing chicken

Side Dishes

Rice or flour tortillas
Fresh fruit

Fast-Food Kitchen Tip

-◈ Use precubed chicken.

-◈ Use prechopped onion.

-◈ Use Crock-Pot liner to limit cleanup.

-◈ Put ingredients into Crock-Pot the night
  before to save time in the morning.

Double-Duty Cooking Tip

-◈ Cut extra chicken into cubes and freeze in
  1-lb. portions.

-◈ Chop 1 extra onion and freeze unused
  portion.

Comment

-◈ Remember to wash hands thoroughly
  after handling raw chicken. Clean any
  area where chicken was handled with hot,
  sudsy water.

❧ Ground Turkey Noodle Casserole ❧

Prep Time: 15–20 minutes

Total Cooking Time: 25 minutes

Fast-Food Meal Prep Time: 7–10 minutes

Serves: 6 generously

Approximate Calories per Serving: 450

Ingredients

1 pkg. (8 oz.) medium or wide egg noodles

1 lb. ground turkey

2 cans (8 oz. each) tomato sauce

1 pkg. (8 oz.) cream cheese, room
   temperature

1 cup cottage cheese

¼ cup sour cream

¼–½ cup minced green onion

1 T. minced green bell pepper

Method

Cook noodles according to package
directions, adding 1 T. of butter or oil to the
water; drain, but do not rinse.

Brown ground turkey in a skillet. Drain
excess fat. Stir in tomato sauce and remove
from heat. Beat cream cheese until smooth;
blend in cottage cheese, sour cream, green
onion, and green pepper.

Spread half of noodles over bottom of baking
dish; cover with cheese mixture and then
remaining noodles. Top with meat sauce.
Bake at 350° for 20–25 minutes.

Tools Needed

9 x 13-inch casserole dish

Skillet

Saucepan

Mixing bowl

Strainer

Measuring cups

Measuring spoons

Can opener

Side Dishes

Green salad or green beans

Rolls

Fast-Food Kitchen Tip

⊁ Use prechopped onion and bell pepper.

⊁ Use precooked ground turkey.

⊁ Use preprepared pasta.

Double-Duty Cooking Tip

⊁ Brown 1 extra lb. of ground turkey and
   freeze in a FoodSaver bag for use later.

⊁ Double the amount of pasta you prepare.
   Set half aside in a strainer. Rinse and
   cool. Store in a FoodSaver bag in the
   refrigerator. To refresh, simply pour hot
   water over pasta through a strainer.

Ham and Tater Tot Casserole

Prep Time: 15 minutes

Total Cooking Time: 45 minutes

Fast-Food Meal Prep Time: 7–10 minutes

Serves: 4 generously

Approximate Calories per Serving: 400

Ingredients
1 pkg. tater tots
1 can cream of chicken soup
¾ cup milk
½ cup mayonnaise
1 cup fully cooked ham, chopped into small bite-sized pieces
1 cup grated cheddar cheese

Method
Bake the tater tots according to package directions in a 9 x 13-inch greased casserole dish. Combine the soup, milk, mayonnaise, and whisk until smooth and creamy. Pour soup mixture and ham over the cooked tater tots. Bake in the oven at 350° for 30 minutes. Sprinkle cheese over the top during the last 10 minutes.

Tools Needed
9 x 13-inch casserole pan
Measuring cups
Mixing bowl
Whisk
Paring knife
Can opener

Side Dishes
Steamed broccoli
Rolls

Fast-Food Kitchen Tip
- Use prechopped ham.
- Use preshredded cheddar cheese.
- Assemble all ingredients except the tater tots and cheese the night before; cover tightly. Everything is ready to assemble the next day for cooking.

Double-Duty Cooking Tip
- When chopping ham, chop extra and freeze in a FoodSaver bag for use later in another recipe.
- Shred extra cheese and freeze in a FoodSaver bag for use later in another recipe.

❧ Hamburger Cups ☙

Prep Time: 15 minutes

Total Cooking Time: 15 minutes

Fast-Food Meal Prep Time: 5 minutes

Serves: 4–5

Approximate Calories per Serving: 250

Ingredients
1 lb. lean ground beef
½ cup barbecue sauce
1 can refrigerator biscuits
¾ cup grated cheddar cheese

Method
Brown ground beef and drain well. Add barbecue sauce, mix well, and set aside. Place biscuits in an ungreased muffin pan, 1 biscuit per muffin cup. Press the biscuit dough up the sides of the cup to the top edge. Spoon barbecue beef mixture evenly into cups. Sprinkle cheddar cheese on top of each muffin cup. Bake at 400° for 12–14 minutes.

Tools Needed
Muffin pan
Measuring cups
Bowl
Spoon

Side Dishes
Potato chips
Fresh fruit

Fast-Food Kitchen Tip
⇥ Use previously prepared frozen ground beef. Thaw or defrost in microwave oven.

⇥ Use preshredded cheese from freezer or refrigerator.

Double-Duty Cooking Tip
⇥ Cook 2 pounds of ground beef and place in FoodSaver bags for later use. (Remember, 2 cups of cooked ground beef equals 1 lb. of ground beef.)

⇥ Make up ground beef packages with barbecue sauce added in. Store in FoodSaver bags and freeze.

⇥ Shred extra cheese and freeze for later use.

❧ Hawaiian Pork Crock-Pot Sandwiches ❧

Prep Time: 15 minutes
Total Cooking Time: 8–9 hours
Fast-Food Meal Prep Time: 7 minutes

Serves: 10–12 generously
Approximate Calories per Serving: 400

Ingredients

1 boneless pork shoulder roast, trimmed, approximately 3 lbs.
2 tsp. olive oil
1 cup onion, chopped fine
½ cup unsweetened pineapple juice
¾ cup teriyaki sauce, plus ¾ cup for adding after pork is cooked
Hamburger buns
Pineapple slices (use juice for recipe)

Method

Cut roast in half or thirds and place in Crock-Pot. Combine olive oil, onion, ¾ cup teriyaki sauce and pineapple juice, whisk together, and pour over roast. Cook on low for 8–9 hours. Take roast out and shred with a fork. Return to Crock-Pot and add additional teriyaki sauce to taste. Heat through.

Spoon approximately ½ cup meat onto each hamburger bun. Top with pineapple slice.

Tools Needed

Crock-Pot
Measuring spoons
Measuring cups
Can opener
Knife

Side Dishes

Potato chips
Fresh fruit

Fast-Food Kitchen Tip

⊸ Reheat frozen Hawaiian Pork in Crock-Pot for 30–45 minutes until heated through. Can also be reheated in microwave oven or on the stove top.

⊸ Use prechopped onion.

Double-Duty Cooking Tip

⊸ After shredding cooked pork and adding extra teriyaki sauce, divide in half and save for a fast-food meal later in the month. Cool before freezing. Freeze in a freezer bag or freezer container.

⊸ Chop extra onion and freeze for later use.

Comment

⊸ Can be served on hamburger buns or in flour tortillas.

❧ Italian Chicken Oregano ❧

(Baked or Crock-Pot)

Prep Time: 15 minutes

Total Cooking Time: 6–8 hours (Crock-Pot)
or 1½ hours (oven)

Fast-Food Meal Prep Time: 5 minutes

Serves: 4 generously

Approximate Calories per Serving: 425

Ingredients
4 boneless, skinless, chicken breasts
1 T. oregano
1 tsp. garlic salt
1 stick (½ cup) butter, melted

Method
Put chicken breasts in Crock-Pot. Place butter, oregano, and garlic salt together in a microwavable bowl. Put in microwave oven on high for 15 seconds or until melted. Stir until blended. Pour over the chicken and turn Crock-Pot on low for 6–8 hours.

This recipe can be baked covered in the oven at 325° for 1½ hours or until chicken is no longer pink. Uncover for last 15 minutes of cooking time.

Tools Needed
Crock-Pot or 8 x 8-inch casserole dish
Microwave-safe bowl for melting butter
    and spices
Measuring cups
Measuring spoons
Whisk

Side Dishes
Rice
Green salad
Rolls

Fast-Food Kitchen Tip
➢ Use premeasured frozen package of chicken and marinade. Set out the night before to thaw. Can be thawed in the Crock-Pot or casserole dish ready to cook.

Double-Duty Cooking Tip
➢ Double or triple recipe and place chicken breasts and marinade in FoodSaver bags and freeze. Can freeze 2 or 4 breasts and marinade depending on the size of your family.

Last-Minute Barbecue Chicken Sandwiches

Prep Time: 15 minutes

Total Cooking Time: 10 minutes

Fast-Food Meal Prep Time: 8 minutes

Serves: 4

Approximate Calories per Serving: 375

Ingredients

4 hamburger buns

2 cans chicken breast meat, drained

¼–½ cup barbecue sauce to taste (choose your favorite)

Method

Drain chicken and place in small saucepan. Add barbecue sauce and heat on low. Toast hamburger buns (toasting optional) and scoop approximately ¼ cup of barbecue chicken mixture on bun.

Optional toppings: Cheese, coleslaw, or jalapeños. Mixture can be heated or reheated in the microwave.

Tools Needed

Small saucepan or microwave-safe dish with lid

Measuring cups

Can opener

Large spoon

Side Dishes

Potato chips or Tater Tots

Corn-on-the-cob

Fruit

Fast-Food Kitchen Tip

⇥ Great meal to serve on busy nights when everyone must be out the door for an activity, meeting, or event. Can be served on paper goods with chips and a pear or apple.

Double-Duty Cooking Tip

⇥ Double or triple the recipe and freeze extra for quick sandwiches on a busy night later in the week. Simply reheat in the microwave in a covered, microwave-safe dish.

Comment

⇥ This is a quick and delicious recipe that is very easy to prepare. You can have all the ingredients on hand for a last-minute meal for busy evenings!

Lemon Chicken over Angel Hair Pasta

Prep Time: 10 minutes

Total Cooking Time: 60 minutes

Fast-Food Meal Prep Time: 5 minutes

Serves: 4–6 generously

Approximate Calories per Serving: 475

Ingredients

3 boneless, skinless chicken breasts

2 T. extra virgin olive oil, divided

¼ cup lemon juice

¼ tsp. garlic powder

Salt and pepper to taste

1 pkg. (16 oz.) angel hair pasta (prepared according to box directions)

Method

Whisk together 1 T. olive oil, lemon juice, garlic powder, and a dash of salt and pepper.

Place the chicken breasts in an 8 x 8-inch glass baking dish. Pour marinade over the top, cover with plastic wrap or foil, and marinate for at least 30 minutes. (This can be done the night before.) Bake the chicken in the oven at 350° for 55–60 minutes or until chicken is done.

Cook pasta according to box directions. Toss with remaining olive oil, salt, and pepper. Slice chicken into strips and place on top of the pasta. You can pour remaining liquid from the cooked chicken over the pasta for a lemony flavor.

Chicken portion of recipe can be prepared in a Crock-Pot. Cook on low for 6–8 hours.

Tools Needed

8 x 8-inch glass baking dish

Saucepan for pasta preparation

Strainer for draining pasta

Measuring cups

Measuring spoons

Side Dishes

Green salad

Steamed broccoli

Fresh or canned fruit

Fast-Food Kitchen Tip

⇥ May be assembled in disposable foil pan to be thrown away after dinner.

⇥ Use Crock-Pot liner to save on cleanup. May be layered in large Crock-Pot the night before, placed in refrigerator to marinate, and cooked the next morning on low for 5–6 hours. Garnish with fresh Parmesan cheese before serving.

⇥ Use prechopped onion and pregrated cheese.

Double-Duty Cooking Tip

⇥ Cook 6 chicken breasts and marinate. Divide in half and freeze chicken and marinade in a large freezer bag or container for another meal later in the month.

Lemon-Lime Citrus Crock-Pot Chicken

Prep Time: 15 minutes

Total Cooking Time: 7–9 hours

Fast-Food Meal Prep Time: 10 minutes

Serves: 4–6 generously

Approximate Calories per Serving: 475

Ingredients

8 boneless, skinless chicken breasts

1 can (6 oz.) frozen lemonade concentrate, thawed to slush consistency

½ cup honey

1 tsp. rubbed sage

½ tsp. ground mustard

½ tsp. dried thyme

½ tsp. lemon juice (fresh or concentrate)

½ tsp. lime juice (fresh or concentrate)

Method

Place fresh or frozen chicken breasts in Crock-Pot. Whisk the remaining ingredients together in mixing bowl. Pour over chicken and cook on low for 8–9 hours.

Optional toppings: Grated cheese, lettuce, avocado slices

Tools Needed

Crock-Pot

Measuring cups

Measuring spoons

Whisk

Mixing bowl

Side Dishes

Coconut rice (Easy coconut rice: Prepare Minute Rice as directed but replace half or full amount of water with canned coconut milk.)

Green salad

Can be served with tortillas to make tacos

Fast-Food Kitchen Tip

⇥ When measuring honey, spray Pam in the measuring cup before adding honey. The honey will slide right out!

⇥ Use Crock-Pot liner for no-mess cleanup.

⇥ Use frozen boneless, skinless chicken breasts.

Double-Duty Cooking Tip

⇥ Double the recipe and set aside half. Cool to room temperature. Store in a FoodSaver bag and freeze for a meal later in the week or month.

✢ Mexican Chicken Quesadillas ✢

Prep Time: 15 minutes

Total Cooking Time: 10 minutes

Fast-Food Meal Prep Time: 7 minutes

Serves: 4 generously

Approximate Calories per Serving: 400

Ingredients

1 chicken breast, (may use canned or frozen) cooked and cut into small chunks

8 flour tortillas

¼ cup onions, finely chopped

¼ cup finely chopped bell pepper (can use green, red, or yellow)

2 T. red or green sauce (optional)

1 cup shredded Mexican cheese (cheddar, mozzarella, and so on; combo)

Method

Preheat oven to 450°. Place four tortillas on a large cookie sheet or baking stone. Sprinkle tortillas with onions and bell pepper evenly. Sprinkle chicken evenly on top of onions and pepper. Sprinkle red or green sauce (if using) evenly on all tortillas and then top with the cheese evenly divided. Cover with remaining tortillas. Bake 8–10 minutes. Cool for 2 minutes and cut with a pizza cutter into pie shaped pieces.

Optional toppings: Sour cream, sliced avocados, and sliced olives

Tools Needed

Cookie sheet or baking stone

Measuring cups

Measuring spoons

Knife or chopper for chopping vegetables

Small cutting board

Side Dishes

Refried beans

Mexican rice

Green salad

Fast-Food Kitchen Tip

➵ Use precooked chicken cubes, canned chicken, or rotisserie chicken (cut into small chunks).

➵ Use prechopped onion and bell pepper.

Double-Duty Cooking Tip

➵ Cook 2 or 3 extra chicken breasts, cube, and freeze in FoodSaver bags for use later in the month.

➵ Chop extra onion and bell pepper and freeze in food-safe containers. Can be stored together for this recipe or individually for use in this or other recipes.

➵ Shred and freeze extra cheese for later use.

Mexican Tortilla Quiche

Prep Time: 15 minutes

Total Cooking Time: 45 minutes

Fast-Food Meal Prep Time: 10 minutes

Serves: 4–6

Approximate Calories per Serving: 400

Ingredients
¾ lb. pork sausage

5 corn tortillas

2 cups shredded Monterey Jack and cheddar cheeses

1 small can chopped green chilies (do not drain)

6 eggs, beaten

½ cup whipping cream

½ cup small curd cottage cheese

½ tsp. chili powder

Method
Brown the sausage until no longer pink; drain well.

In a 9-inch pie plate place 4 of the corn tortillas around the pie plate and let the tortillas extend a little beyond the plate. Put the last tortilla in the middle of the pie plate. Layer the sausage over the tortillas. Add the cheese and green chilies, spreading evenly. Mix together the eggs, cream, cottage cheese, and chili powder. Pour over sausage and cheese. Bake at 350° for 45 minutes. The center should be set before removing. Cut into wedges.

Optional toppings: Sour cream, avocado slices

Tools Needed
Skillet

Pie plate

Measuring cups

Measuring spoons

Mixing bowl

Large spoon

Can opener

Side Dishes
Fresh fruit

Fast-Food Kitchen Tip
- Use precooked sausage.

- Reheat extra frozen quiche in microwave or oven. (Reheat frozen quiche in oven set at 300° for approximately 45–55 minutes or until heated thoroughly.) May be defrosted and reheated in microwave oven if frozen in a microwave-safe dish.

Double-Duty Cooking Tip
- Make extra quiche and cover tightly and freeze for later in the week or month.

- Brown extra serving of sausage and freeze in a FoodSaver bag.

- Shred extra cheese and freeze in a FoodSaver bag.

⚜ Mock Monte Cristo Sandwiches ⚜

(Trader Joe's)

Prep Time: 15 minutes

Total Cooking Time: 10 minutes

Fast-Food Meal Prep Time: 10 minutes

Serves: 3 generously

Approximate Calories per Serving: 325

Ingredients

1 box Trader Joe's Low-Fat French Toast (no preservatives)

6 thin slices, deli-sliced ham

6 thin slices, deli-sliced turkey

3 thin slices, deli-sliced Swiss cheese

1 T. mayonnaise (optional)

1 T. mustard (optional)

1 T. butter

Method

Mix together the mayonnaise and mustard and set aside. Take one slice of French toast and spread with ¼ tsp. of mayonnaise/mustard mixture. Add 2 slices of ham, 1 piece of Swiss cheese, and 2 slices of turkey. Spread ¼ tsp. of mayonnaise/mustard mixture on the other piece of French toast and close sandwich together. Butter the outside of each piece of toast and place on a hot griddle or skillet set to low. Let brown on both sides until cheese melts and deli meats are warm. Dust with powdered sugar. Repeat this method for each sandwich.

Tools Needed

Griddle

Butter knife

Measuring spoon

Side Dishes

Fresh fruit

Fast-Food Kitchen Tip

⇴ Use Trader Joe's Low-Fat French toast.

⇴ Use premixed mayonnaise/mustard mixture.

⇴ Use prestored frozen sandwiches. Just add mayonnaise/mustard mixture and butter. Grill.

Double-Duty Cooking Tip

⇴ Make up 2 extra sandwiches with just the French toast, the meats, and cheese. Flash-freeze (see "Tips" section on page 32 for flash-freeze instructions). Freeze individually in FoodSaver bags. Add mayonnaise/mustard mixture and butter when preparing.

❧ Pasta Turkey Bake ❧

Prep Time: 15 minutes

Total Cooking Time: 60–65 minutes

Fast-Food Meal Prep Time: 10 minutes

Serves: 4 generously

Approximate Calories per Serving: 400

Ingredients

2 cups cooked, cubed turkey (or chicken)

1½ cups uncooked elbow macaroni

2 cups shredded cheddar cheese (8 oz.), divided

1 can condensed cream of chicken soup, undiluted

1 cup milk

Black pepper to taste

1 can mushroom stems/pieces, drained (optional)

Method

Cube turkey or chicken. Combine the meat, uncooked macaroni, 1½ cups cheese, soup, milk, mushrooms, and pepper in a large bowl. Pour into greased 2-quart baking dish. Cover and bake at 350° for 60–65 minutes. Uncover; sprinkle with remaining cheese. Bake 5–10 minutes longer or until cheese is melted.

Ingredients may be combined and put in Crock-Pot. Cook on low 6–8 hours. Add remaining cheese before serving.

Tools Needed

2-quart baking dish or Crock-Pot

Measuring cups

Can opener

Large bowl

Large spoon

Side Dishes

Green salad

Rolls

Fast-Food Kitchen Tip

⤞ Reheat extra cooked portion from storage container or casserole dish.

⤞ Heat uncooked casserole in oven. Take off lid/plastic wrap from casserole dish and cover with foil before placing in the oven. Cook as per recipe directions.

⤞ Use canned turkey or chicken or rotisserie chicken from your local market.

⤞ Use preshredded cheese from the freezer.

Double-Duty Cooking Tip

⤞ Double the recipe and freeze 1 portion (uncooked) in a freezer/oven/microwave-safe dish with a lid. Cover with plastic wrap or aluminum foil before replacing the lid. Can be reheated in the microwave or cooked in the oven.

⤞ Grate extra cheese and place in a FoodSaver bag for use later in another recipe.

Comment

⤞ Great recipe for leftover holiday turkey or extra rotisserie chicken.

✣ Quick and Easy Italian Chicken ✣

Prep Time: 15 minutes

Total Cooking Time: 45 minutes

Fast-Food Meal Prep Time: 15 minutes

Serves: 6 generously

Approximate Calories per Serving: 525

Ingredients

4 cups prepared spaghetti sauce (choose your favorite)

6 frozen, breaded chicken patties

6 slices mozzarella cheese

Method

Preheat oven to 350°. In a 9 x 13-inch glass pan, pour 1 cup of the spaghetti sauce. Place the frozen, breaded chicken patties on top of the sauce. Pour the remaining sauce over the top. Place cheese slices on the chicken (one slice for each piece of chicken). Bake for 30–45 minutes or until chicken is hot and the cheese has melted.

Tools Needed

9 x 13-inch pan

Measuring cup

Side Dishes

Spaghetti (or any favorite pasta)

Green salad

Hot garlic bread

Fast-Food Kitchen Tip

➤ Use this meal for a quick and delicious meal for busy evenings when the family will be out the door for various activities.

➤ Use bagged green salad lettuce.

➤ Use precooked pasta that has been placed in a FoodSaver bag in refrigerator. Refresh by pouring boiling water over the pasta through a strainer.

➤ Use paper goods for quick cleanup.

Double-Duty Cooking Tip

➤ Cook 1 extra portion pasta, cool, and store in a FoodSaver bag in the refrigerator.

☙ Quick Tuna Wrap ☙

Prep Time: 15 minutes
Total Cooking Time: 0 minutes
Fast-Food Meal Prep Time: 10 minutes

Serves: 4 generously
Approximate Calories per Serving: 600 (for one full tortilla)

Ingredients
4 whole wheat flour tortillas
1 small can tuna (white tuna, in water), drained well
2 T. mayonnaise
Fresh spinach
Red, yellow, or orange bell pepper (or a combination of the three) cut into thin strips
Purple onion, cut into thin strips (optional)
Avocado slices (optional)

Method
Put drained tuna in a bowl and mix with mayonnaise. Set aside. Lay out flour tortillas and cover with spinach, leaving approximately ½ inch around the border. Spoon ¼ of the tuna mixture into the center and down the middle of the tortilla. Next add bell pepper strips, onion strips (optional) and avocado slices (optional). Roll 2 ends into the middle, turn and fold. By placing the spinach first, you can roll the wrap tightly, and then wrap with plastic wrap, very tightly, and store for 1–2 days in the refrigerator.

Tools Needed
Paring knife
Butter knife
Measuring spoon

Side Dishes
Potato chips
Fresh fruit

Fast-Food Kitchen Tip
❧ Use pre-prepared tuna.

❧ Use precut vegetables.

Double-Duty Cooking Tip
❧ Make 1 extra can of tuna with mayonnaise mixture. Save half in a FoodSaver bag and refrigerate for up to 1 week.

❧ Cut extra bell pepper and onion strips and place in a FoodSaver bag and refrigerate for up to 1 week.

Slow Cooker Hot "Hamwiches"

Prep Time: 10 minutes

Total Cooking Time: 4–5 hours

Fast Food Meal Cooking Time: 5 minutes

Serves: 10–12 generously

Approximate Calories per Serving: 300

Ingredients
3 lbs. deli ham, sliced thin
2 cups apple juice
⅔ cup packed brown sugar
½ cup sweet pickle relish
2 tsp. prepared mustard
1 tsp. paprika
12 deli rolls, sliced

Method
Separate ham slices and place in a 3-quart slow cooker. In a bowl, whisk together the apple juice, brown sugar, relish, mustard, and paprika. Pour over the ham. Mix to coat the ham.

Cook on low for 4–5 hours or until completely heated through. Place 3–4 slices of ham per sandwich roll. Add additional relish if desired.

Serve with your favorite potato chips. Great meal to enjoy outdoors!

Tools Needed
Crock-Pot
Measuring cups
Measuring spoons

Side Dishes
Potato chips
Potato salad
Fresh fruit

Fast-Food Kitchen Tip
↠ Use premeasured marinade.

↠ Use Crock-Pot liner to eliminate messy cleanup.

Double-Duty Cooking Tip
↠ When measuring ingredients for the marinade, make 1 extra recipe amount and freeze in a food-safe bowl for use in this recipe later in the month.

❧ Spanish Style Beef and Bean Stew ❧

Prep Time: 15 minutes
Total Cooking Time: 8–9 hours
Fast-Food Meal Prep Time: 10 minutes

Serves: 6–8 generously
Approximate Calories per Serving: 520

Ingredients
1½ lb. stew meat, cut into 1-inch cubes
1 T. vegetable oil
16 oz. beef broth
1 cup chunky salsa (your favorite)
1 medium to large onion, chopped
1 garlic clove, minced (or ¼ tsp. garlic
     powder)
1 can (15 oz.) pinto beans, rinsed and drained
1 can (16 oz.) whole kernel corn, drained
2 T. chili powder
1 tsp. ground cumin

Method
Place cubed beef in the Crock-Pot with the
vegetable oil. Stir until beef is coated. Mix
together the beef broth, chunky salsa, onion,
garlic, beans, corn, chili powder, and cumin.
Pour over beef. Cover and cook on low for
8–9 hours. Meat should be fork tender.

Tools Needed
Crock-Pot
Measuring spoons
Large mixing bowl
Large spoon
Can opener

Side Dishes
Green salad
Fresh fruit
Rolls

Fast-Food Kitchen Tip
❧ Use prechopped onion.

❧ Use precubed beef.

Double-Duty Cooking Tip
❧ Buy 3 lbs. of stew meat and cut into cubes.
   Freeze half of the cubed stew meat in a
   FoodSaver bag for use in this or another
   recipe in the next 2 months.

❧ Chop an extra onion and freeze half in a
   FoodSaver bag for use in another recipe.

Veggies, Sides, and Salads

❧ Amazing Marinade ❧

Prep Time: 10 minutes

Total Cooking Time: 0 minutes

Fast-Food Meal Prep Time: 10 minutes

Approximate Calories per Serving: 50

Ingredients

2 cups lemon-lime soda

1 cup soy sauce

½ cup olive oil

½ tsp. garlic powder

½ tsp. prepared horseradish

Method

Mix ingredients together and store in an airtight bowl. Use to marinate chicken (must be marinated overnight). Chicken can be marinated, then frozen. Cook chicken in a skillet or on the barbecue grill.

Tools Needed

Mixing bowl

Measuring cups

Measuring spoons

Whisk

Airtight bowl for storing marinade

Fast-Food Kitchen Tip

⇥ Use premarinated and frozen chicken for a quick meal on the barbecue grill.

Double-Duty Cooking Tip

⇥ Make up 2 batches and store extra in a suitable container and freeze.

⇥ Marinate 4 chicken breasts overnight and freeze in a FoodSaver bag for a meal later in the week or month. When freezing marinated chicken, drain off extra marinade before freezing.

❧ Artichoke Dip ❧

Prep Time: 15 minutes

Total Cooking Time: 20–25 minutes

Fast-Food Meal Prep Time: 10 minutes

Serves: 8–10 generously

Approximate Calories per Serving: 45

Ingredients

2 cans artichoke hearts, rinsed, drained, and chopped

1 can diced green chilies

2 tsp. finely ground garlic

1 cup mayonnaise

1 cup Parmesan cheese

Method

Mix together the chopped artichokes, green chilies, garlic, mayonnaise, and cheese. Mix well. Pour into an 8 x 8-inch casserole dish sprayed with cooking spray. Bake at 350° for 20–25 minutes or until bubbly.

Tools Needed

8 x 8-inch pan

Measuring cups

Measuring spoons

Can opener

Mixing bowl

Large spoon

Side Dishes

Serve with chips, crackers, or bread

Fast-Food Kitchen Tip

↬ Use pregrated cheese.

↬ Use pre-prepared uncooked, frozen artichoke dip. Thaw and bake.

Double-Duty Cooking Tip

↬ Make a double batch and freeze half in an 8 x 8-inch casserole dish, uncooked. Wrap tightly and cover with a lid (if available). Otherwise, cover with plastic wrap first, and then cover with aluminum foil. Use within 2 months.

❧ Chocolate Chip Cheese Ball ❧

By Becky Barnard

Prep Time: 15 minutes

Total Cooking Time: 0 minutes

Fast-Food Meal Prep Time: 10 minutes

Serves: 10–12 generously

Approximate Calories per Serving: 250–400
   (depending on how much you eat!)

Ingredients

1 pkg. (8 oz.) cream cheese, softened to room
   temperature

½ cup butter (1 stick), softened to room
   temperature (no substitutes)

¼ tsp. vanilla extract

¾ cup confectioner's sugar (powdered sugar)

2 T. brown sugar

¾ cup semisweet chocolate chips

Chopped pecans (optional)

Method

With a hand mixer, beat cream cheese, butter,
and vanilla until fluffy. Add in sugars and
mix by hand. Add chocolate chips and
mix by hand. Put mixture in refrigerator
for 1 hour. Take out and roll into a ball and
place in waxed paper and put back in the
refrigerator for another hour. Take out and
roll in chopped pecans (if desired).

Serve with graham crackers or graham
cracker sticks. This is a great recipe for buffets
and holiday gatherings.

Tools Needed

Hand mixer

Bowls

Measuring cups

Measuring spoons

Large spoon for mixing

Fast-Food Kitchen Tip

⊸ Place butter, cream cheese, and vanilla in
   a covered bowl and set out 2 hours ahead
   of preparation to soften.

⊸ Mix together both sugars and chocolate
   chips in a separate bowl, ready to add to
   cream cheese mixture.

⊸ Can be assembled while you are working
   in the kitchen on another meal.

Double-Duty Cooking Tip

⊸ Prepare an extra cheese ball and wrap tight
   in waxed paper. Flash-freeze for 2 hours
   and then place in FoodSaver bag and
   refrigerate. You can reshape before serving.

⊸ You can make up several during the
   holiday season to have on hand for parties
   and dessert get-togethers or to serve to
   surprise guests.

❖ Easy Herb Biscuits ❖

Prep Time: 15 minutes

Total Cooking Time: 15 minutes

Fast-Food Meal Prep Time: 5–7 minutes

Serves: 6–8 generously

Approximate Calories per Serving: 250

Ingredients

1 pkg. Pillsbury biscuits

½ cup (1 stick) butter, melted

½ tsp. thyme

½ tsp. sage

½ tsp. garlic powder

Method

Mix together the thyme, sage, and garlic powder; add to melted butter and mix thoroughly.

Cut each biscuit into quarters in pie-shaped wedges with kitchen scissors.

Dip each quarter in the butter and herbs mixture. Bake at 300° for approximately 15 minutes or until golden brown.

Tools Needed

Cookie sheet

Kitchen scissors

Small bowl

Measuring spoon

Fast-Food Kitchen Tip

⤙ Use premeasured butter mixture. If frozen, thaw to room temperature and warm in the microwave.

Double-Duty Cooking Tip

⤙ When measuring butter and herbs, triple the amount and store in 1 or 2 small freezer containers and freeze for use again later for this recipe.

❧ Parmesan Asparagus ❧

Prep Time: 15 minutes

Total Cooking Time: 10 minutes

Fast-Food Meal Prep Time: 10 minutes

Serves: 4–6 generously

Approximate Calories per Serving: 225

Ingredients

1 T. butter

¼ cup extra virgin olive oil

1 lb. fresh trimmed asparagus spears

¾ cup grated Parmesan cheese

Salt and pepper to taste (coarsely ground pepper is delicious!)

Method

In a large skillet, melt the butter and the olive oil together. Add asparagus spears and cook on medium heat, stirring occasionally for about 7–10 minutes. When desired firmness is reached, drain off excess oil and sprinkle with salt and pepper. Sprinkle Parmesan cheese right before serving.

Tools Needed

Large skillet

Measuring cups

Measuring spoons

Large spoon

Fast-Food Kitchen Tip

⇥ Use pregrated Parmesan cheese.

⇥ Use pretrimmed asparagus.

Double-Duty Cooking Tip

⇥ Wash and trim extra asparagus and store in a FoodSaver bag in the refrigerator for up to 2 weeks for use later for another meal.

Ranch-Style Potato Salad

Prep Time: 15–20 minutes

Total Cooking Time: 20 minutes

Fast-Food Meal Prep Time: 10 minutes

Serves: 10–12 generously

Approximate Calories per Serving: 475

Ingredients
4–5 lbs. small red potatoes, unpeeled
1 lb. cooked bacon, crumbled
¾ cup green onion, chopped
2 pkgs. ranch dressing mix
1 cup mayonnaise
1 cup sour cream
1 small can sliced olives, drained well

Tools Needed
Extra large saucepan
Large serving bowl
Small bowl
Measuring cups
Measuring bowls
Large spoon
Can opener

Method
Bring a pot of water to a boil and salt lightly. Add whole red, unpeeled potatoes. Cook until tender, 15–20 minutes. Drain and run potatoes under cool tap water. Chop into 1-inch cubes. Transfer cubed potatoes to a large serving bowl. Refrigerate until completely chilled, at least 2 hours. In a small mixing bowl, mix together the ranch dressing mix, mayonnaise, sour cream, olives, and green onions. Cover and chill overnight. Cook bacon until crisp, put between paper towels to absorb grease. Let sit until cool. Put bacon in a baggie and take a rolling pin and crush bacon. Stir dressing mixture into bowl of cooled, cubed potatoes. Add the bacon right before serving.

Fast-Food Kitchen Tip
- Use precooked and crushed bacon.
- Use prechopped green onion.
- Use premixed dressing.

Double-Duty Cooking Tip
- Cook extra bacon and freeze in a suitable container for use in a recipe later in the week or month.
- Chop an extra bunch of green onions and freeze in a FoodSaver bag.
- Mix up 1 extra batch of dressing and store in the refrigerator for up to 1 week.

❧ Spicy Muffins ❧

Prep Time: 15 Minutes

Total Cooking Time: 20 minutes

Fast-Food Meal Prep Time: 10 minutes

Serves: 8–10 generously

Approximate Calories per Serving: 275

Ingredients
1 box Jiffy corn bread mix
2 cups creamed corn
1 small can chopped green chilies
1 tsp. sugar
1 egg
½ cup shredded cheddar cheese (optional)

Method
Mix well and spoon into cupcake muffin pan lined with cupcake papers. Bake according to Jiffy package directions. Sprinkle with cheese after removing from the oven.

Tools Needed
Muffin pan
Cupcake papers
Measuring cups
Measuring spoon
Large spoon
Small bowl
Can opener

Fast-Food Kitchen Tip
⇥ Use preshredded cheddar cheese.

⇥ Thaw frozen muffins and warm in the microwave using the defrost/thaw setting. Cover the muffins with a damp paper towel before re-warming.

Double-Duty Cooking Tip
⇥ Make a double batch, flash freeze, and place in a FoodSaver bag.

⇥ Shred extra cheese and freeze in a FoodSaver bag.

Summertime Pasta Salad

Prep Time: 15 minutes

Total Cooking Time: 15 minutes

Fast-Food Meal Prep Time: 10 minutes

Serves: 4 generously

Approximate Calories per Serving: 475

Ingredients
1 box (16 oz.) bow-tie pasta, cooked as
directed. (Drain thoroughly, but do
not rinse.)
4 fresh tomatoes, diced
2 cloves garlic, finely diced
2 T. purple onion, finely chopped
4 T. extra virgin olive oil
½ tsp. white vinegar
2 cups mozzarella cheese, grated

Method
Cook the pasta as per package directions.
Drain, but do not rinse. Set aside and keep
warm.

Mix together the tomatoes, garlic, onion,
virgin olive oil, and vinegar. Toss this mixture
with the pasta and quickly add the cheese
while the pasta is warm so that it will melt.
Serve warm. Add chicken for a complete meal.

Tools Needed
Saucepan
Large mixing bowl
Large spoon
Measuring cups
Measuring spoons
Knife
Strainer

Side Dishes
To make a complete meal, add shredded
leftover rotisserie chicken.
Rolls
Fresh fruit

Fast-Food Kitchen Tip
⇥ Use preminced garlic.

⇥ Use prechopped purple onion.

⇥ Use pregrated cheese.

⇥ Use precooked pasta. Refresh by pouring
boiling water over the pasta through a
strainer.

Double-Duty Cooking Tip
⇥ Shred extra mozzarella cheese and store in
a FoodSaver bag and freeze.

⇥ Chop extra purple onion and store in a
FoodSaver bag and freeze.

⇥ Cook extra serving of pasta, drain (do
not rinse), and cool to room temperature.
Store in a FoodSaver bag and keep in the
refrigerator for use later in the week or
month.

Desserts

Chocolate Fudge Peanut Butter Crock-Pot Cake

Prep Time: 15 minutes

Total Cooking Time: 1½–2 hours in
    Crock-Pot

Fast-Food Meal Prep Time: 7 minutes

Serves: 8–12

Approximate Calories per Serving:
375–400

Ingredients

¼ plus ½ cup sugar (divided)
½ cup all-purpose flour
¾ tsp. baking powder
⅓ cup milk
¼ cup peanut butter
1 T. vegetable oil
½ tsp. vanilla extract
2 T. baking cocoa
1 cup boiling water

Method

In a medium bowl, combine ¼ cup of the sugar, flour, and baking powder. In another bowl, combine the milk, peanut butter, oil, and vanilla. Stir this mixture into the dry mixture until combined. Don't over-mix. Spray nonstick cooking spray into 3-quart Crock-Pot. Spread this mixture evenly into the Crock-Pot.

In another bowl combine the cocoa and ½ cup sugar; stir in the boiling water. Pour this mixture into the Crock-Pot on top of other mixture. *Do not stir.* Cover and cook on high for 1½–2 hours or until a toothpick inserted near the center comes out clean. Serve warm

with your favorite ice cream or whipped topping, and sprinkle with nuts (optional).

Tools Needed

Crock-Pot
2 bowls
Large spoon for mixing
Measuring spoons
Measuring cups

Fast-Food Kitchen Tip

- Use premeasured dry ingredients for quick assembly.

Double-Duty Cooking Tip

- In a suitable storage container, measure out 2–3 extra portions of flour, ¼ cup sugar, and baking powder for making this recipe at a later time. In a separate container, measure out 2–3 extra portions of cocoa and ½ cup sugar for making this recipe at a later time.

Comment

- Spray measuring cup with nonstick cooking spray before measuring the peanut butter. It will come out with ease.

❧ Chocolate Gravy ❧

By Donna Clegg

Prep Time: 10 minutes

Total Cooking Time: 10–15 minutes

Fast-Food Meal Prep Time: 5 minutes

Serves: 6–8 generously

Approximate Calories per Serving: 300

Ingredients

2 heaping T. all-purpose flour

2 level T. cocoa

¾–1 cup sugar

Dash of salt

2 cups milk

Method

Mix all ingredients together in a medium saucepan over medium heat until thickened. Serve warm over buttered biscuits, English muffins, or buttered toast. This recipe comes from Donna's grandma—she made this sauce often during the Great Depression.

Tools Needed

Medium-sized saucepan

Large spoon

Measuring cups

Measuring spoons

Side Dishes

Serve sauce over buttered biscuits, English muffins, or buttered toast.

Fast-Food Kitchen Tip

⤙ Use premeasured dry ingredients.

⤙ Use frozen gravy. Reheat in saucepan or in the microwave (use microwave-safe dish).

Double-Duty Cooking Tip

⤙ When measuring the dry ingredients, make 2 extra portions and put in suitable containers. Can be stored in the pantry or refrigerator.

⤙ Make a double batch of the gravy and freeze in a large freezer container.

❧ Chocolate Nut Crunch ❧

Prep Time: 10 minutes

Total Cooking Time: 20 minutes

Fast-Food Meal Prep Time: 15 minutes

Serves: 4 generously

Approximate Calories per Serving: 400

Ingredients
½ cup walnuts, chopped
¾ cup brown sugar, packed
½ cup butter
1 cup chocolate chips

Method
Sprinkle nuts over bottom of lightly greased 8 x 8-inch pan. Combine sugar and butter in saucepan; bring to a rolling boil, stirring constantly. Boil 4–6 minutes or until temperature reaches 270°. Pour over nuts in pan. Sprinkle with chips. Cover for 2 minutes; evenly spread melted chips. Chill until firm. Remove from pan; break into pieces.

Tools Needed
8 x 8-inch pan
Measuring cups

❧ Cinnamon Tortilla Cookies ❧

Prep Time: 10 minutes

Total Cooking Time: 6 minutes

Fast-Food Meal Prep Time: 5 minutes

Serves: 4–6 generously

Approximate Calories per Serving (per 8 cookies): 150

Ingredients

2 T. cinnamon
½ cup sugar
6 flour tortillas (small taco size)
Pam cooking spray (original or butter flavor)

Method

In a small bowl, mix together sugar and cinnamon, set aside.

Using kitchen scissors or pizza cutter, cut the flour tortillas into wedges. Lay them single layer on a cookie sheet and spray with Pam. Bake in a preheated oven at 350 ° for approximately 3 minutes. Watch carefully to make sure they don't burn. Take them out, flip them over, and spray with Pam. Bake for 3 minutes. Take them out of the oven and sprinkle with sugar mixture immediately. Serve warm with milk.

Tools Needed

Cookie sheet
Kitchen scissors
Measuring spoon
Measuring cup

Fast-Food Kitchen Tip

⊰ Have all ingredients on hand for a quick last-minute snack for kids or to serve with coffee or hot tea when friends drop by.

Double-Duty Cooking Tip

⊰ Cut 1 or more extra sets of tortillas and put in a FoodSaver bag or other container for your next batch.

⊰ Measure several servings of brown sugar and cinnamon and put in small freezer containers. Can be frozen or refrigerated.

⅙ Coconut Angel Whip ⅙

Prep Time: 15 minutes

Total Cooking Time: 60 minutes

Fast-Food Meal Prep Time: 15 minutes

Serves: 8–12 generously

Approximate Calories per Serving: 450

Ingredients

1 pkg. Jell-O vanilla instant pudding
   (4-serving size)

1 can (20 oz.) crushed pineapple, in its own
   juice, undrained

1 cup coconut

1 cup Cool Whip (thawed in refrigerator)

1 round angel food cake (from mix or store
   bought)

Fresh strawberries, sliced, or chunk pineapple
   pieces

Method

In a large bowl, mix dry pudding with crushed pineapple and the juice. Add coconut and stir into pudding mixture. Fold Cool Whip in gently.

Slice angel food cake horizontally and evenly to make three "disks." Place first disk, cut side up and spoon one-third of the pudding mixture onto the cake. Add second layer and repeat with filling. Repeat with the last layer of cake. Spread mixture evenly and top with strawberries and/or pineapple chunks. Refrigerate until firm and cold. Can be frozen before slicing and serving for a cool and delicious treat!

Tools Needed

Large mixing bowl

Large spoon or spatula

Measuring cup

Plate

Fast-Food Kitchen Tip

⇥ Prepare the cake the night before and cover tightly. Refrigerate overnight.

Double-Duty Cooking Tip

⇥ Keep ingredients on hand for a quick dessert idea.

⇥ Preslice strawberries.

⇥ Premeasure cake mixture ingredients and store in the refrigerator. Assemble the next day.

Dangerous Five-Minute Mug Chocolate Cake

Prep Time: 10 minutes

Total Cooking Time: 3 minutes

Fast-Food Meal Prep Time: 5 minutes

Serves: 1–2

Approximate Calories per Serving: 475

Ingredients

4 T. flour

4 T. sugar

2 T. cocoa

3 T. chocolate chips (optional)

1 tsp. chopped walnuts or pecans (optional)

1 egg

3 T. milk

3 T. oil

Splash of vanilla extract

1 large coffee mug (microwave safe)

Method

Spray coffee mug with Pam cooking spray. Add dry ingredients to coffee mug and mix well. Add the egg and mix thoroughly. Pour in the milk and oil and mix together well. Add the vanilla. Put the mug in the microwave and cook for 3 minutes on high (1000 watts). The cake will rise over the top of the mug, but don't be alarmed! Allow to cool a little, and tip out onto a plate if desired.

Frost if desired and serve with a scoop of ice cream. Can be served with a dollop of Cool Whip. This can serve 2 if you are feeling generous.

And why is this the most dangerous cake recipe in the world? Because now you are only 5 minutes away from chocolate cake at any time of the day or night! Enjoy!

Tools Needed

Large coffee mug(s)

Measuring spoons

Spoon for stirring ingredients

Fast-Food Kitchen Tip

- This recipe is a quick and fun dessert to keep on hand for surprise guests. Takes less than 5 minutes to assemble and cook.

Double-Duty Cooking Tip

- Assemble three extra sets of dry ingredients into coffee mugs and cover with plastic wrap. Store in the refrigerator.

- Assemble extra sets of dry ingredients in small freezer containers and freeze.

❧ Grilled Pineapple Surprise ❧

Prep Time: 10 minutes

Total Cooking Time: 15 minutes

Fast-Food Meal Prep Time: 5 minutes

Serves: 4–8

Approximate Calories per Serving: 250

Ingredients

Fresh pineapple, cut in thick slices and cored

⅛ tsp. cayenne pepper

2 T. honey (or agave nectar sweetener)

Method

Mix cayenne pepper and honey together in a small bowl and set aside. Place pineapple on a clean, greased grill (use a stove top griddle or the barbecue grill) and cook until grill marks appear, turning frequently, approximately 4–5 minutes. Brush with honey and spice mixture and turn 2 more times. Take off the grill and serve with a small scoop of vanilla bean ice cream and mint sprigs for garnish (optional). Delicious!

Tools Needed

Stove top griddle (or outside barbecue grill)

Paring knife

Measuring spoons

Small bowl

Pastry brush

Side Dishes

Serve with 1 scoop of real vanilla bean ice cream.

Fast-Food Kitchen Tip

⤞ Use canned pineapple slices, drained.

Double-Duty Cooking Tip

⤞ Pour pineapple juice (from canned pineapple) into ice cube tray and freeze. Place frozen cubes in a FoodSaver bag and store in freezer. Great for making juice smoothies!

Pretzel Pecan Bites

by Amy Schumacher

Prep Time: 15 minutes

Total Cooking Time: 10 minutes

Fast-Food Meal Prep Time: 10 minutes

Approximate Calories per Serving: 85

Ingredients

Pretzels (you will need to use the pretzels that are twist-shaped)

Rolo chocolate/caramel candies

Pecan halves

Method

Preheat oven to 250°. Place pretzels on cookie sheet and add one Rolo candy on the top of each pretzel. Do not press down yet.

Cook for 4–5 minutes. Take out of oven and press pecan half on top of each pretzel. Let cool. Can be refrigerated after they cool. They can also be frozen.

Tools Needed

Cookie sheet

Fast-Food Kitchen Tip

⊣ Pull out frozen candies and defrost.

⊣ Use frozen unwrapped candies for quicker assembly.

Double-Duty Cooking Tip

⊣ Keep candy, pretzels, and pecans on hand.

⊣ Unwrap candies and keep in a freezer bag or container in the freezer.

⊣ Make a double batch and freeze half in a large container to have on hand.

Comment

⊣ These are great to have on hand for a quick snack, when unexpected guests drop by, or an after school snack for kids. The sweet and savory flavor makes them a great hit!

Quick and Yummy Chocolate Tomato Soup Cake

Prep Time: 10 minutes

Total Cooking Time: 30–35 minutes

Fast-Food Meal Prep Time: 10 minutes

Serves: 4 generously

Approximate Calories per Serving: 400

Ingredients

1 box chocolate cake mix (any brand, approximately 18 oz.)

1 can (10¾ oz.) tomato soup (undiluted)

1 tsp. baking soda

2 eggs

Method

Grease and flour cake pan(s). Pour cake mix into a large bowl. Add undiluted tomato soup, baking soda, and eggs. Mix well. Follow baking directions on back of cake mix box. Sprinkle with powdered sugar, frosting, or for a quick and kid-friendly frosting, cover the top of the cake with marshmallows just after you remove it from the oven so the marshmallows will melt on the hot cake.

Tools Needed

Mixing bowl

Large mixing spoon

9 x 13-inch cake pan or two round cake pans

Measuring spoons

Fast-Food Kitchen Tip

➤ Keep ingredients on hand for a quick dessert.

Double-Duty Cooking Tip

➤ Prepare cake in a 9 x 13-inch dish, cool and cut in half. Frost and serve one half. Flash-freeze the other half and freeze in a FoodSaver bag for another day. Defrost in refrigerator or on counter top. Frost as desired.

✣ Quick Peach Cobbler—Trader Joe's ✣

By Christine Dunham

Prep Time: 15 minutes

Total Cooking Time: 30 minutes

Fast-Food Meal Prep Time: 10 minutes

Serves: 8–12

Approximate Calories per Serving: 525

Ingredients

8 fresh peaches, peeled; or 8 fresh nectarines, unpeeled; or frozen peaches

1 cup sugar

Cinnamon (to taste—approximately ¼–½ tsp.)

Nutmeg (to taste—approximately ¼–½ tsp.)

1 tub Mascarpone cheese* (found at Trader Joe's)

1 T. honey

½ cup heavy whipping cream

1 box Trader Joe's vanilla wafers

May substitute 1 cup crème fraîche (Trader Joe's), cream cheese, or Greek yogurt for the Mascarpone cheese.

Method

Cook peaches (or nectarines) and sugar in a saucepan for 20–30 minutes. Add the cinnamon and nutmeg and set aside. Whisk together the mascarpone cheese, honey, and heavy whipping cream. Set aside.

In a 9 x 13-inch casserole pan, layer the bottom with a single layer of vanilla wafer cookies. Then layer the peach mixture, followed by the cream mixture. Top with crumbled cookies. Serve warm with vanilla bean ice cream.

Tools Needed

9 x 13-inch pan

Measuring cups

Measuring spoons

Paring knife

Saucepan

Mixing bowl

Large spoon

Whisk

Side Dishes

Vanilla bean ice cream

Fast-Food Kitchen Tip

⇥ Use frozen peaches or nectarines.

Double-Duty Cooking Tip

⇥ Cook double batch of peaches (or nectarines) with sugar and spices and set aside half. Freeze in a large freezer container for use in this recipe later in the month.

WEEKLY MENU PLANNER

Week of: _____

Day of Week	BREAKFAST	LUNCH	DINNER
MONDAY	DD ☐ FF ☐ PG ☐	DD ☐ FF ☐ PG ☐	DD ☐ FF ☐ PG ☐
TUESDAY	DD ☐ FF ☐ PG ☐	DD ☐ FF ☐ PG ☐	DD ☐ FF ☐ PG ☐
WEDNESDAY	DD ☐ FF ☐ PG ☐	DD ☐ FF ☐ PG ☐	DD ☐ FF ☐ PG ☐
THURSDAY	DD ☐ FF ☐ PG ☐	DD ☐ FF ☐ PG ☐	DD ☐ FF ☐ PG ☐
FRIDAY	DD ☐ FF ☐ PG ☐	DD ☐ FF ☐ PG ☐	DD ☐ FF ☐ PG ☐
SATURDAY	DD ☐ FF ☐ PG ☐	DD ☐ FF ☐ PG ☐	DD ☐ FF ☐ PG ☐
SUNDAY	DD ☐ FF ☐ PG ☐	DD ☐ FF ☐ PG ☐	DD ☐ FF ☐ PG ☐

DD = Double-Duty Cooking   FF = Fast Food Meal   PG = Use paper goods

WEEKLY MENU PLANNER

Week of: _____

Day of Week	BREAKFAST	LUNCH	DINNER
MONDAY	DD ☐ FF ☐ PG ☐	DD ☐ FF ☐ PG ☐	DD ☐ FF ☐ PG ☐
TUESDAY	DD ☐ FF ☐ PG ☐	DD ☐ FF ☐ PG ☐	DD ☐ FF ☐ PG ☐
WEDNESDAY	DD ☐ FF ☐ PG ☐	DD ☐ FF ☐ PG ☐	DD ☐ FF ☐ PG ☐
THURSDAY	DD ☐ FF ☐ PG ☐	DD ☐ FF ☐ PG ☐	DD ☐ FF ☐ PG ☐
FRIDAY	DD ☐ FF ☐ PG ☐	DD ☐ FF ☐ PG ☐	DD ☐ FF ☐ PG ☐
SATURDAY	DD ☐ FF ☐ PG ☐	DD ☐ FF ☐ PG ☐	DD ☐ FF ☐ PG ☐
SUNDAY	DD ☐ FF ☐ PG ☐	DD ☐ FF ☐ PG ☐	DD ☐ FF ☐ PG ☐

DD = Double-Duty Cooking   FF = Fast Food Meal   PG = Use paper goods

✣ About the Author ✣

Sheri Torelli is a nationally recognized conference speaker and owner/director of More Hours in My Day. Emilie Barnes and Sheri met in 1981 and have worked together since that time. Sheri and her husband, Tim, are in partnership with Bob and Emilie Barnes, founders of More Hours in My Day. Sheri is the co-author of *More Hours in My Day* and *Your Simple Guide to a Home-Based Business*. Her articles appear in *Chicken Soup* as well as magazines and newsletters.

Based in Riverside, California, Sheri travels and speaks to women across the country for conferences, retreats, special events, and seminars. Sheri teaches the More Hours in My Day organizational seminars and writes a weekly e-mail subscription newsletter.

If you are interested in booking a seminar or speaking event, please contact:

Sheri Torelli
More Hours in My Day
2150 Whitestone Drive
Riverside, CA 92506

(951) 682-4714

Website: www.emiliebarnes.com
E-mail: sheri@emiliebarnes.com